# A TURKISH WOMAN'S
# EUROPEAN IMPRESSIONS

ZEYNEB IN HER PARIS DRAWING-ROOM
She is wearing the Yashmak and Feradjé, or cloak.

# CAMBRIDGE LIBRARY COLLECTION

*Books of enduring scholarly value*

## European History

This series includes accounts of historical events and movements by eye-witnesses and contemporaries, as well as landmark studies that assembled significant source materials or developed new historiographical methods. It covers the social and political history of continental Europe from the Renaissance to the end of the nineteenth century, and its broad range includes works on Russia and the Balkans, revolutionary France, the papacy and the inquisition, and the Venetian state archives.

## A Turkish Woman's European Impressions

Zeyneb Hanoum (who died *c.* 1923) and her sister Melek fled Turkey in 1906, at a time when women's freedom was severely restricted. This book, first published in 1913, is a collection of letters written by Zeyneb to her friend, feminist journalist Grace Ellison. As well as discussing the political situation in Turkey, Hanoum compares the life of Turkish women with their European counterparts and presents a more balanced view of real harem life. Witty and forthright, the author shares her opinions on strange Western phenomena such as tennis, snobbery and the poor quality of English food. She also offers views on the suffragette movement and muses on the freedoms enjoyed by women in the West. The author's outsider status provides fascinating insights into European culture and such diverse experiences as tea at the House of Commons and bullfighting. This remains an entertaining and touching travelogue from a unique viewpoint.

Cambridge University Press has long been a pioneer in the reissuing of out-of-print titles from its own backlist, producing digital reprints of books that are still sought after by scholars and students but could not be reprinted economically using traditional technology. The Cambridge Library Collection extends this activity to a wider range of books which are still of importance to researchers and professionals, either for the source material they contain, or as landmarks in the history of their academic discipline.

Drawing from the world-renowned collections in the Cambridge University Library and other partner libraries, and guided by the advice of experts in each subject area, Cambridge University Press is using state-of-the-art scanning machines in its own Printing House to capture the content of each book selected for inclusion. The files are processed to give a consistently clear, crisp image, and the books finished to the high quality standard for which the Press is recognised around the world. The latest print-on-demand technology ensures that the books will remain available indefinitely, and that orders for single or multiple copies can quickly be supplied.

The Cambridge Library Collection brings back to life books of enduring scholarly value (including out-of-copyright works originally issued by other publishers) across a wide range of disciplines in the humanities and social sciences and in science and technology.

# A Turkish Woman's European Impressions

ZEYNEB HANOUM
EDITED BY GRACE ELLISON

CAMBRIDGE
UNIVERSITY PRESS

CAMBRIDGE UNIVERSITY PRESS

Cambridge, New York, Melbourne, Madrid, Cape Town,
Singapore, São Paolo, Delhi, Mexico City

Published in the United States of America by Cambridge University Press, New York

www.cambridge.org
Information on this title: www.cambridge.org/9781108050470

© in this compilation Cambridge University Press 2012

This edition first published 1913
This digitally printed version 2012

ISBN 978-1-108-05047-0 Paperback

# A TURKISH WOMAN'S
# EUROPEAN IMPRESSIONS

BY

ZEYNEB HANOUM

(HEROINE OF PIERRE LOTI'S NOVEL
"LES DÉSENCHANTÉES")

EDITED & WITH AN INTRODUCTION BY
GRACE ELLISON

WITH 23 ILLUSTRATIONS
FROM PHOTOGRAPHS & A DRAWING BY
AUGUSTE RODIN

LONDON
SEELEY, SERVICE & CO. LTD.
38 GREAT RUSSELL STREET
1913

# CONTENTS

CONTENTS

# ILLUSTRATIONS

# INTRODUCTION

IN the preface of his famous novel, *Les Désen-chantées*, M. Pierre Loti writes: "This novel is pure fiction; those who take the trouble to find real names for Zeyneb, Melek, or André will be wasting their energy, for they never existed."

These words were written to protect the two women, Zeyneb and Melek, who were mainly responsible for the information contained in that book, from the possibility of having to endure the terror of the Hamidian régime as a consequence of their indiscretion. This precaution was unnecessary, however, seeing that the two heroines, understanding the impossibility of escaping the Hamidian vigilance, had fled to Europe, at great peril to their lives, before even the novel appeared.

Although it is not unusual to find Turkish women who can speak fluently two or three European languages (and this was very striking to me when I stayed in a Turkish harem), and although M. Loti has in his novel taken the

precaution to let Melek die, yet it would still
have been an easy task to discover the identity
of the two heroines of his book.

Granddaughters of a Frenchman who for
*les beaux yeux* of a Circassian became a Turk
and embraced Mahometanism, they had been
signalled out from amongst the enlightened
women who are a danger to the State, and
were carefully watched.

For a long time many cultured Turkish
women had met to discuss what could be done
for the betterment of their social status; and
when it was finally decided to make an appeal
to the sympathy of the world in the form of a
novel, who better than Pierre Loti, with his
magic pen and keen appreciation of Turkish
life, could be found to plead the cause of the
women of what he calls his " second fatherland " ?

In one of my letters written to Zeyneb from
Constantinople, I hinted that the Young Turks
met in a disused cistern to discuss the Revolution
which led Europe to expect great things of them.
The women, too, met in strange places to plot
and plan—they were full of energetic inten-
tions, but, with the Turkish woman's difficulty
of bringing thought into action, they did little

more than plot and plan, and but for Zeyneb and Melek, *Les Désenchantées* would never have been written.

At the conclusion of his preface, M. Loti says: " What is true in my story is the culture allowed to Turkish women and the suffering which must necessarily follow.    This suffering, which to my foreign eyes appeared perhaps more intense, is also giving anxiety to my dear friends the Turks themselves, and they would like to alleviate it. The remedy for this evil I do not claim to have discovered, since the greatest thinkers of the East are still diligently working to find it."

Like M. Loti I, too, own my inability to come any nearer a solution of this problem.    I, who through the veil have studied the aimless, un-healthy existences of these pampered women, am nevertheless convinced that the civilisation of Western Europe for Turkish women is a case of exchanging the frying-pan for the fire.    Zeyneb in her letters to me, written between 1906–1912, shows that, if her disenchantment with her harem existence was bitter, she could never appreciate our Western civilisation.

Turkish women are clamouring for a more solid education and freedom.    They would cast aside˙ the hated veil; progress demands they should—but do they know for what they are asking ?

"Be warned by us, you Turkish women," I said to them, painting the consequences of our freedom in its blackest colours, "and do not pull up your anchor till you can safely steer your ship. My own countrymen have become too callous to the bitter struggles of women ; civilisation was never meant to be run on these lines, therefore hold fast to the protection of your harems till you can stand alone."

Since my return to London, I have sometimes spoken on Turkish life, and have been asked those very naïve questions which wounded the pride of Zeyneb Hanoum. When I said I had actually stayed in an harem, I could see the male portion of my audience, as it were, passing round the wink. "You must not put the word 'harem' on the title of your lecture," said the secretary of a certain society. "Many who might come to hear you would stay away for fear of hearing improper revelations, and others would come hoping to hear those revelations and go away disappointed."

In one of her letters to me, Zeyneb complains that the right kind of governess is not sent to Constantinople. The wonder to me is, when one hears what a harem is supposed to be, that European women have the courage to go there at all.

The word harem comes from the Arabic " Maharem," which means " sacred or for- bidden," and no Oriental word has been more misunderstood. It does not mean a collection of wives ; it is simply applied to those rooms in a Turkish house exclusively reserved for the use of the women. Only a blood relation may come there to visit the lady of the house, and in many cases even cousins are not admitted. There is as much sense in asking an Englishman if he has a boudoir as in asking a Turk if he has a harem ; and to think that when I stayed in Turkey, our afternoon's impropriety consisted of looking through the latticed windows ! The first Bey who passed was to be for me, the second for Fathma, and the third for Selma ; this was one of our favourite games in the harem. One day I remember in the country we waited an hour for my Bey to pass, and after all he was not a Bey, but a fat old man carrying water.

The time has not yet come for the Turkish woman to vindicate her right to freedom ; it cannot come by a mere change of law, and it is a cruelty on the part of Europeans to encourage

B

them to adopt Western habits which are a part of a general system derived from a totally different process of evolution.

In the development of modern Turkey, the Turkish woman has already played a great part, and she has a great part still to play in the creation of a new civilisation; but present experience has shown that no servile imitation of the West will redeem Turkey from the evils of centuries of patriarchal servitude.

.        .        .        .        .        .

By a strange irony of fate, it was at Fontainebleau that I first made the acquaintance of Pierre Loti's heroines. To me every inch of Fontainebleau was instinct with memories of happiness and liberty. It was here that Francis I. practised a magnificence which dazzled Europe; here, too, is the wonderful wide forest of trees which are still there to listen to the same old story. . . . From a Turkish harem to Fontainebleau. What a change indeed!

The two sisters were sitting on the verandah of their villa when I arrived. Zeyneb had been at death's door; she looked as if she were there still.

" Why did you not come to lunch ? " asked Melek.

" I was not invited," I answered.

" Well, you might have come all the same."

" Is that the custom in Turkey ? "

" Why, of course, when you are invited to lunch you can come to breakfast instead, or the meal after, or not at all. Whenever our guests arrive, it is we who are under obligations to them for coming."

" What a comforting civilisation ; I am sure I should love to be in Turkey."

I wanted to ask indiscreet questions.

" Have you large trees in Turkey with hollows big enough to seat two persons ? " I began.

Melek saw through the trick at once.

" Ah ! " she answered, " now you are treading on dangerous ground ; next time you come to see us we shall speak about these things. In the meanwhile learn that the charming side of life to which you have referred, and about which we have read so much in English novels, does not exist for us Turkish women. Nothing in our life can be compared to yours, and in a short time you will see this. We have no right to vary ever so little the programme arranged for us by the customs of our country ; an adventure of any kind generally ends in disaster. As you may know, we women never see our husbands till we are married, and an unhappy marriage is none the less awful to bear when it is the work of some one else."

" Do tell me more," I persisted.

" The marriage of a Turkish woman is an intensely interesting subject to anyone but a Turkish woman. . . . "

.    .    .    .    .    .

I left my new friends with reluctance, but after that visit began the correspondence which forms the subject matter of this book.

GRACE ELLISON.

# CHAPTER I

## A DASH FOR FREEDOM

# A TURKISH WOMAN'S EUROPEAN IMPRESSIONS

## CHAPTER I

### A DASH FOR FREEDOM

A FEW days after my visit to the Désenchantées at Fontainebleau, which is described
in the Introduction, I received the following
letter from Zeyneb :

FONTAINEBLEAU, *Sept.* 1906.

You will never know, my dear and latest
friend, the pleasure your visit has given us. It
was such a new experience, and all the more to
be appreciated, because we were firmly convinced we had come to the end of new
experiences.

For almost a quarter of a century, in our dear
Turkey, we longed above all for something new ;
we would have welcomed death even as a change,
but everything, everything was always the same.

And now, in the space of eight short months, what have we not seen and done ! Every day has brought some new impressions, new faces, new joys, new difficulties, new disappointments, new surprises and new friends ; it seemed to both of us that we must have drunk the cup of novelty to its very dregs.

On Sunday, after you had left us, we talked for a long time of you and the many subjects we had discussed together.

Sympathy and interest so rarely go hand in hand—interest engenders curiosity, sympathy produces many chords in the key of affection, but the sympathetic interest you felt for us has given birth on our side to a sincere friendship, which I know will stand the test of time.

We felt a few minutes after you had been with us, how great was your comprehension, not only of our actions, but of all the private reasons, alas ! so tragic, which made them necessary. You understood so much without our having to speak, and you guessed a great deal of what could not be put into words. That is what a Turkish woman appreciates more than anything else.

We, who are not even credited with the possession of a soul, yet guard our souls as our most priceless treasures. Those who try to force our confidence in any way, we never forgive. Between friend and friend the highest form of sympathy is silence. For hours we Turkish women sit and commune with one another without speaking. You would, I know, understand this beautiful side of our life.

Since our departure from our own country, and during these few months we have been in France, from all sides we have received kindness. We were ready to face yet once more unjust criticism, blame, scandal even ; but instead, ever since we left Belgrade till we arrived here, everything has been quite the opposite. All the European papers have judged us impartially, some have even defended and praised us, but not one censured us for doing with our lives what it pleased us.

But in Turkey what a difference ! No Constantinople paper spoke of our flight. They were clever enough to know that by giving vent to any ill-feeling, saying what they really thought of our " disgraceful " conduct, they would draw still more attention to the women's cause ; so we were left by the Press of our country severely alone.

The Sultan Hamid, who interested himself a

little too much in our welfare, became very anxious about us. Having left no stone unturned to force us to return (he had us arrested in the middle of the night on our arrival at Belgrade on the plea that my sister was a minor, and that both of us had been tricked away by an elderly lady for illicit purposes) he next ordered that all those European papers in which we were mentioned should be sent to him. As our flight drew forth bitter criticism of his autocratic government, he must, had he really taken the trouble to read about us, have found some very uncomfortable truths about himself. But that was no new régime. For years he has fed himself on these indigestible viands, and his mechanism is used to them by now.

I need not tell you that in Constantinople, for weeks, these forbidden papers were sold at a high price. Regardless of the risk they were running, everyone wanted to have news of the two women who had had the audacity to escape from their homes and the tyranny of the Sultan Hamid. In the harems, we were the one topic of conversation. At first no one seemed to grasp the fact that we had actually gone, but when at last the truth slowly dawned upon them, the men naturally had not a kind word to say of us, and we did not expect it would be otherwise. But the women, alas! Many were obliged officially to disapprove of our action. There were a few, however, who had the courage to defend us openly; they have our deepest and sincerest gratitude. But do not think for a moment that we blame or feel unkindly towards the others. Have not we, like them, had all our lives to suffer and fear and pretend as captives always must do? Could they be expected to find in one day the strength of character to defend a cause however just, and not only just, but *their own*—their freedom.

Yes, my friend, we ourselves have lived that life of constant fear and dissimulation, of hopes continually shattered, and revolt we dared not put into words.

Yet never did the thought occur to us that we might adapt ourselves to this existence we were forced to lead. We spent our life in striving for one thing only—the means of changing it.

Could we, like the women of the West, we thought, devote our leisure to working for the poor, that would at least be some amusement to break the monotony. We also arranged to meet and discuss with intelligent women the question of organising charity, but the Sultan came down upon us with a heavy hand.   He saw the danger of allowing thinking women to meet and talk together, and the only result of this experiment was that the number of spies set to watch the houses of " dangerous women " was doubled.

Then it was that we made up our minds, after continual failure, that as long as we remained in our country under the degrading supervision of the Hamidian régime, we could do nothing, however insignificant, to help forward the cause of freedom for women.

I need not tell you again all the story of our escape; it is like a nightmare to me still, and every detail of that horrible journey will remain clearly fixed in my mind until death.   Shall I tell you all that has happened to us since ? But so much has been said about us by all sorts and conditions of men and women, that you will no doubt have already had an overdose.   Yet I thought I understood, from the sympathetic interest you showed us the other afternoon, that there was much you would still like to hear. Have I guessed rightly ?   Then there is nothing you shall not know.—Your affectionate

ZEYNEB.

What a long and interesting letter ! and from a Turkish woman too ! Several times I read and re-read it, then I felt that I could not give my new friend a better proof of the pleasure that it had given me, than by writing her at once to beg for more.   But I waited till the next day, and finally sent a telegram—" Please send another letter."

# CHAPTER II

## ZEYNEB'S GIRLHOOD

# CHAPTER II

## ZEYNEB'S GIRLHOOD

Fontainebleau, *Sept.* 1906.

WHEN I was quite young I loved to read the history of my country told in the Arabian Nights style. The stories are so vivid and picturesque, that even to-day, I remember the impression my readings made on me. [Alas ! the profession of *conteur* or *raconteur* is one which has been left behind in the march of time.] Formerly every Pasha had a *conteur*, who dwelt in the house, and friends were invited from all around to come and listen to his Arabian Nights stories. The tales that were most appreciated were those which touched on tragic events. But the stories contained also a certain amount of moral reflection, and were told in a style which, if ever I write, I will try to adopt. The sentences are long, but the rhythm of the well-chosen language is so perfect that it is almost like a song.

What a powerful imagination had these men !

C

And how their stories delighted me! There were stories of Sultans who poisoned, Ministers who were strangled, Palace intrigues which ended in bloodshed, and descriptions of battles where conqueror and conquered were both crowned with the laurels of a hero. But I never for a moment thought of these tales but as fiction! Could the history of any country be so awful! Yet was not the story of the reign in which I was living even worse, only I was too young to know it ? Were not the awful Armenian massacres more dreadful than anything the *conteurs* had ever described ? Was not the bare awful truth around us more ghastly than any fiction ? Indeed, it was.

How can I impress upon your mind the anguish of our everyday life; our continual and haunting dread of what was coming; no one could imagine what it means except those Turkish women who, like ourselves, have experienced that life.

Had we possessed the blind fatalism of our grandmothers, we should probably have suffered less, but with culture, as so often happens, we began to doubt the wisdom of the Faith which should have been our consolation.

You will say, that I am sad—morbid even;

A TURKISH CHILD WITH A SLAVE

Until a Turkish girl is veiled, she leads the life of an ordinary European child. She even goes to Embassy balls. This is a great mistake, as it gives her a taste for a life which after she is veiled must cease.

A TURKISH HOUSE

The Harem windows are on the top floor to the right.

but how can I be otherwise when the best years of my life have been poisoned by the horrors of the Hamidian régime. There are some sentiments which, when transplanted, make me suffer even as they did in the land of my birth. I am thinking particularly of the agony of waiting.

Do you think there is in any language a sentence stronger and more beautiful than that which terminates in Loti's *Pêcheurs d'Islande*—the tragedy of waiting—with these words, " Il ne revint jamais " ?

I mention this to you because my whole youth had been so closely allied with this very anguish of waiting.

Imagine for a moment a little Turkish Yali [1] on the shores of the Bosphorus. It is dark, it is still, and for hours the capital of Turkey has been deep in slumber. Scarcely a star is in the sky, scarcely a light can be seen in the narrow and badly-paved streets of the town.

I had been reading until very late—reading and thinking, thinking and reading to deaden the uneasiness I always felt when something was going to happen. What was coming this time ?

---

[1] Yali = a little summer residence resorted to when it is too hot to remain in Constantinople itself.

By a curious irony of fate, I had been reading in the Bible [1] of Christ's apostles whose eyes were heavy with sleep. But I could not sleep, and after a time I could not even read. This weary, weary waiting!

So I rose from my bed and looked through my latticed windows at the beautiful Bosphorus, so calm and still, whilst my very soul was being torn with anguish. But what is that noise? What is that dim light slowly sailing up the Bosphorus? My heart begins to beat quickly, I try to call out, my voice chokes me. The caïque has stopped at our Yali.

Now I know what it is. Four discreet taps at my father's window, and his answer " I am coming." Like a physician called to a dying patient, he dresses and hastily leaves the house. It is three o'clock in the morning *à la Franque*,[2] but his master is not sleeping. Away yonder, in his fortress of Yildiz, the dreaded Sultan trembles even more than I. What does he want

[1] The Turkish women with whom I lived in Constantinople read the Bible by the advice of the Imam (the Teacher of the Koran) to help them in the better understanding of the Koran. I may add that Zeyneb's knowledge of our Scriptures, and her understanding of Christ's teaching, would put to shame many professing Christians in our Western Churches.

[2] French time.

with my father ? Will he be pacified this time as he has often been before ? What if my father should have incurred the wrath of this terrible Sultan ? The caïque moves away as silently as it came. Will my beloved father ever return ? There is nothing to do but to go on waiting, waiting.

.    .    .    .    .

Let us change the scene. A Turkish official has arrived at our house, he has dared to come as far as the very door of the harem. He is speaking to my mother.

"I am only doing my duty in seeing if your husband is here ? I have every right to go up those harem stairs which you are guarding so carefully, look in all your rooms and cupboards. My duty is to find out where your husband is, and to report to his Majesty at once."

This little incident may sound insignificant to you, yet what a tragedy to us ! What was to happen to the bread-winner of our family ? What had my beloved father done ?

The explanation of it was simple enough. A certain Pasha had maligned him to the Sultan in a most disgraceful manner. And the Sultan might have believed it, had he not, by the merest chance, discovered that my father was at the

Palace when the Pasha so emphatically said he was elsewhere.  On such slender evidence, the fate of our family was to be weighed !  Would it mean exile for our father ?  Would we ever see him any more ?  Again I say, there was nothing to do but wait.

.    .    .    .    .    .

As we told you on Sunday, we Turkish women read a great deal of foreign literature, and this does not tend to make us any more satisfied with our lot.

Amongst my favourite English books were Beatrice Harraden's *Ships that Pass in the Night*,[1] passages of which I know by heart, and Lady Mary Montagu's *Letters*.  Over and over again, and always with fresh interest, I read those charming and clever letters.  Although they are the letters of another century, there is nothing in them to shock or surprise a Turkish woman of to-day in their criticism of our life. It is curious to notice, when reading Lady Mary's *Letters*, how little the Turkey of to-day differs from the Turkey of her time ; only, Turkey, the child that Lady Mary knew, has grown into a big person.

[1] When I asked a Turkish friend to write in my album, to my surprise and pride she wrote from memory a passage from *Ships that Pass in the Night*.

There are two great ways, however, in which we have become too modern for Lady Mary's book. In costume we are on a level with Paris, seeing we buy our clothes there ; and as regards culture, we are perhaps more advanced than is the West, since we have so much leisure for study, and are not hampered with your Western methods. And yet how little we are known by the European critics !

The people of the West still think of us women as requiring the services of the public letter-writer ! They think of us also—we, who have so great an admiration for them, and interest ourselves in all they are doing—as one amongst many wives. Yet Polygamy (and here I say a *Bismillah* [1] or prayer of thankfulness) has almost ceased to exist in Turkey.

I know even you are longing to make the acquaintance of a harem, where there is more than one wife, but to-day the number of these establishments can be counted on five fingers. We knew intimately the wife of a Pasha who had more than one wife. He was forty years old, a well-known and important personage, and in his Palace beside his first wife were many slave-

---

[1] Prayer which all devout Moslems say before beginning a work.

wives; the number increased from year to year. But again I repeat this is an exception.

We used often to visit the poor wife, who since her marriage had never left her home, her husband being jealous of her, as he was of all the others; they were *his possessions*, and in order to err on the safe side, he never let them out.

Our friend, the first wife, was very beautiful, though always ailing. Every time we went to see her, she was so grateful to us for coming, thanked us over and over again for our visit, and offered us flowers and presents of no mean value. And she looked so happy, continually smiling, and was so gentle and kind to all her *entourage*.

She told our mother, however, of the sorrow that was gnawing at her heart-strings, and when she spoke of the Pasha she owned how much she had suffered from not being the favourite. She treated her rivals with the greatest courtesy. " It would be easy to forgive," she said, " the physical empire that each in turn has over my husband, but what I feel most is that he does not consult me in preference to the others."

She had a son fifteen years old, whom she loved very dearly, but she seemed to care for the fourteen other children of the Pasha quite as much, and spoke of them all as " our children." Although her husband had bought her as a slave, she had a certain amount of knowledge too, and she read a great deal in the evenings when she was alone, alas ! only too often.

The view of the Bosphorus, with the ships coming and going, was a great consolation to her, as it has been to many a captive.  And she thanked Allah over and over again that she at least had this pleasure in life.

I have often thought of this dear, sweet woman in my many moments of revolt, as one admires and reverences a saint, but I have never been able to imitate her calm resignation.

Unlike our grandmothers, who accepted without criticism their " written fate," we analysed our life, and discovered nothing but injustice and cruel, unnecessary sorrow.  Resignation and culture cannot go together.  Resignation has been the ruin of our country.  There never would have been all this suffering, this perpetual injustice, but for resignation ; and resignation was no longer possible for us, for our Faith was tottering.

But I am not really pitying women more

than men under the Hamidian régime. A
man's life is always in danger. Do you know,
the Sultan was informed when your friend
Kathleen came to see us ? Every time our
mother invited guests to the house, she was
obliged to send the list to his Majesty, who, by
every means, tried to prevent friends from
meeting. Two or three Turks meeting together
in a café were eyed with suspicion, and reported
at head-quarters, so that rather than run risks
they spent the evenings in the harems with their
wives. One result, however, of this awful
tyranny, was that it made the bonds which
unite a Turkish family together stronger than
anywhere else in the world.

Can you imagine what it is to have detectives
watching your house day and night ? Can
you imagine the exasperation one feels to think
that one's life is at the mercy of a wretched
individual who has only to invent any story
he likes and you are lost ? Every calumny,
however stupid and impossible, is listened to
at head-quarters. The Sultan's life-work (what
a glorious record for posterity !) has been to
have his poor subjects watched and punished.
What his spies tell him he believes. No trial is

necessary, he passes sentence according to his temper at the moment—either he has the culprit poisoned, or exiles him to the most unhealthy part of Arabia, or far away into the desert of Tripoli, and often the unfortunate being who is thus punished has no idea why he has been condemned.

I shall always remember the awful impression I felt, when told with great caution that a certain family had disappeared. The family consisted of the father, the mother, son and daughter, and a valet. They were my neighbours—quiet, unobtrusive people—and I thought all the more of them for that reason.

One morning, when I looked out of my window, I saw my neighbour's house was closed as if no one lived there. Without knowing what had happened to them, I became anxious, and discreetly questioned my eunuch, who advised me not to speak about them. It appeared, however, that in the night the police had made an inspection of the house, and no one has since then heard of its occupants, or dared to ask, for fear of themselves becoming " suspect."

I found out long after, from a cutting sent me

from a foreign friend in Constantinople, that
H. Bey's house had been searched, and the
police—and this in spite of the fact that he
had been forbidden to write—had found there
several volumes of verses, and he was condemned to ten years' seclusion in a fortified
castle at Bassarah.

This will perhaps give you some idea of the
conditions under which we were living.  Constant fear, anguish without hope of compensa-
tion, or little chance of ever having anything
better.

That we preferred to escape from this life, in
spite of the terrible risks we were running, and
the most tragic consequences of our action, is
surely comprehensible.

If we had been captured it would only have
meant death, and was the life we were leading
worth while ?  We had taken loaded revolvers
with us, to end our lives if necessary, remembering the example of one of our childhood friends,
who tried to escape, but was captured and taken
back to her husband, who shut her up till the
end of her days in a house on the shores of the
Marmora.

You have paid a very pretty compliment to

our courage.   Yet, after all, does it require very
much to risk one's life when life is of so little
value ?   In Turkey our existence is so long, so
intolerably long, that the temptation to drop a
little deadly poison in our coffee is often too
great to withstand.   Death cannot be worse
than life, let us try death.—Your affectionate
                                                ZEYNEB.

# CHAPTER III

## BEWILDERING EUROPE

# CHAPTER III

## BEWILDERING EUROPE

WHAT a curious thing it was I found so much difficulty in answering Zeyneb's letters. To send anything *banal* to my new friend I felt certain was to run the risk of ending the correspondence.

She knew I was in sympathy with her ; she knew I could understand, as well as any one, how awful her life must have been, but to have told her so would have offended her. Most of the reasons for her escape, every argument that could justify her action, she had given me, except one; and it was probably that " one " reason that had most influenced her.

In due time probably she would tell me all, but if she did not, nothing I could do or say would make her, for Turkish women will not be cross-examined. One of them, when asked one day in a Western drawing-room " how many wives has your father ? " answered, without hesitation, " as many as your husband, Madame."

49

D

Zeyneb had once told me that I succeeded in guessing so much the truth of what could not be put into words.  She had on one occasion said " we never see our husbands until we are married," and a little later " sometimes the being whose existence we have to share inspires us with a horror that can never be overcome." Putting these two statements together, I was able to draw my own conclusions as to the " one " reason. . . . Poor little Zeyneb !

It seemed to me from the end of her letter, that Zeyneb would have been grateful had I said that I approved of her action in leaving her own country.  To have told her the contrary would not have helped matters in the least, and sooner or later she was sure to find out her mistake for herself.

And who that noticed her enthusiasm for all she saw would have dreamt of the tragedy that was in her life ?  The innocent delight she had when riding on the top of a bus, and her jubilation at discovering an Egyptian Princess indulging in the same form of amusement !

Zeyneb told me that *economy* was a word for which there was no equivalent in the Turkish language, so how could she be expected to practise an art which did not exist in her country ?

It was from her I had learnt the habit of answering her letters by telegram, and the result had been satisfactory. " Eagerly waiting for another letter," I wired her. The following letter arrived :

FONTAINEBLEAU, *Oct.* 1906.

A few days after our arrival began in earnest a new experience for us. The " demands " for interviews from journalists—every post brought a letter. Many reporters, it is true, called without even asking permission ; wanted to know our impressions of West Europe after eight days ; the reasons why we had left Turkey; and other questions still more ignorant and extraordinary about harem life.

When, however, we had conquered the absurd Oriental habit of being polite, we changed our address, and called ourselves by Servian names.

What an extraordinary lack of intelligence, it seemed, to suppose that in a few phrases could be related the history of the Turkish woman's evolution ; and the psychology of a state of mind which forces such and such a decision explained. How would it have been possible to give the one thousand and one private reasons connected with our action ! And what would

be the use of explaining all this to persons one
hoped never to see again—persons by whom
you are treated as a spectacle, a living spectacle,
whose adventures will be retailed in a certain
lady's boudoir to make her " five o'clock " less
dull ?

" What made you think of running away
from Turkey ? " asked one of these press detectives.  He might as well have been saying
to me, " You had on a blue dress the last time
I saw you, why are you not wearing it
to-day ? "

" Weren't you sorry to leave your parents ? "
asked another.  Did he suppose because we
were Turks that we had hearts of stone.  How
could anyone, a complete stranger too, dare to
ask such a question ?   And yet, angry as I was,
this indiscretion brought tears to my eyes, as
it always does when I think of that good-bye.

" Good night, little girl," said my father, on
the eve of our departure.   " Don't be so long in
coming to dine with us again.   Promise that you
will come one day next week."

I almost staggered.   " I'll try," I answered.
Every minute I felt that I must fling myself in
his arms and tell him what I intended to do,
but when I thought of our years and years of

suffering, my mind was made up, and I kept
back my tears.

Do you see now, dear Englishwoman, why we
appreciated your discreet interest in us, and how
we looked forward to a friendship with you who
have understood so well, that there can be
tears behind eyes that smile, that a daughter's
heart is not necessarily hard because she breaks
away from the family circle, nor is one's love for
the Fatherland any the less great because one
has left it forever ?   All this we feel you have
understood, and again and again we thank you.—
Your affectionate                ZEYNEB.

FONTAINEBLEAU, *Oct.* 1906.

You ask me to give you my first impression
of France (wrote Zeyneb), but it is not so
much an impression of France, as the impression of being free, that I am going to write.
What I would like to describe to you is the
sensation of intense joy I felt as I stood for the
first time before a window wide open that had
neither lattice-work nor iron bars.

It was at Nice.   We had just arrived from
our terrible journey.   We had gone from hotel
to hotel, but no one would give us shelter even
for a few hours.   Was that Christian charity, to

refuse a room because I was thought to be dying ? I cannot understand this sentiment. A friend explained that a death in an hotel would keep other people away. Why should the Christians be so frightened of death ?

I was too ill at the moment to take in our awful situation, and quite indifferent to the prospect of dying on the street. Useless it was, however, our going to any more hotels ; it was waste of time and waste of breath, and I had none of either to spare. No one advised us, and no one seemed to care to help us, until, by the merest chance, my sister remembered our friends in Belgrade had given us a doctor's address. We determined to find him if we possibly could. In half an hour's time we found our doctor, who sent us at once to a sanatorium. There they could not say, " You are too ill to come in," seeing illness was a qualification for admittance. But I shall not linger on those first moments in Europe : they were sad beyond words.

It must have been early when I awoke the next morning, to find the sun forcing its way through the white curtains, and flooding the whole room with gold. Ill as I was, the scene was so beautiful that I got out of bed and opened wide

the window, and what was my surprise to find
that there was no lattice-work between me and
the blue sky, and the orange trees, and the hills
of Nice covered with cypress and olives ?    The
sanatorium garden was just one mass of flowers,
and their sweet perfume filled the room.    With
my eyes I drank in the scene before me, the
hills, and the sea, and the sky that never seemed
to end.

A short while after, my sister came in.    She
also from her window had been watching at the
same time as I.    But no explanation was necessary.    For the first time in our lives we could
look freely into space—no veil, no iron bars.    It
was worth the price we had paid, just to have
the joy of being before that open window.    I
sign myself in Turkish terms of affection.—
Your carnation and your mouse,

ZEYNEB.

# CHAPTER IV

### SCULPTURE'S FORBIDDEN JOY

# CHAPTER IV

## SCULPTURE'S FORBIDDEN JOY—
## M. RODIN AT HOME

ZEYNEB and Melek left Fontainebleau and travelled to Switzerland by short stages; their first halting-place was Paris.

They stayed for a week in the gay capital, and during that time Melek and I visited some of the principal churches and monuments.

" Sight-seeing " was what the Hanoums [1] then called " freedom." To them it meant being out of the cage; tasting those pleasures which for so many years had been forbidden. Their lesson was yet to be learnt.

We went one afternoon to see M. Rodin. Rising, summer and winter, at a very early hour, the sculptor had finished the greater part of his work for the day when we arrived; the model was resting, and he was talking with the students, who had come to discuss their difficulties with him.

[1] Hanoum = Turkish lady.

To me this opportunity given to young talent of actually seeing a master at work was such a happy idea, I made the remark to M. Rodin.

" If only those who succeed," he said, " be it in the difficult accomplishment of their daily task, or in the pursuit of some glorious end, had the courage to speak of their continual efforts, their struggles, and their suffering, what a glorious lesson in energy it would be for those who were striving for a place amongst the workers.

" Those who have arrived should say to those who are starting : At each corner, there is suffering ; at each turning some fresh struggle begins, and there is sorrow all the time. We who have conquered have passed by that road, you can go no other way.

" But when once they have got to their destination, the successful men are silent. And they who are still on the way get tired of the daily toil, knowing not that they who have arrived, have had the very same experience."

Many beautiful works attracted our attention that afternoon, the most striking being Mary Magdalene, in repentant anguish at the feet of her Master, Jesus ; the Prodigal Son with his hands clasped in useless regret towards a wasted

LES DÉSENCHANTÉES
From a sketch by Auguste Rodin.

and ill-spent life. Then there was a nude (I forget the name by which she will be immortalised), her wonderful arms in a movement of supplication, so grand, that the Eastern woman and I together stretched out our hands towards it in appreciation.

The sculptor saw our movement, understood and thanked us ; a few moments later, conscious of our action, we blushed. What had we done ?

I, the Scotch puritan, had actually admired one of those beautiful nudes before which we, as children, shut our eyes. But the Oriental ?

" In my country these marble figures are not seen," she explained, " 'the face and form created by God must not be copied by man,' said our Prophet, and for centuries all good Moslems have obeyed this command."

" Do you know the legend of the Prophet's son-in-law Osman ? " she said.

" No," I answered, " please tell me."

" One day, long, long ago," related Melek, " when the followers of Christ had left their church, Osman entered and broke all the sacred images except one. Then when he had finished his work of destruction, he placed his axe at the foot of the figure he had left intact.

" The next day, the Christians discovering

what had happened, tried to find the guilty person. Osman's air of calm triumph betrayed him.

" ' What have you done ? ' they cried, rushing towards him.

" ' Nothing,' he answered, ' I am innocent ; it is your Divinity who has destroyed everything.'

" ' Our Divinity cannot move.'

" ' If your Divinity is lifeless,' answered Osman, ' why do you pray to a God of stone ? ' [1]

. . . . . .

" In the Meandre valley in Asia," went on Melek, " the sculptured heads on the tombs are cursed. At Ephesus and Herapolis the Turcomans turn away in horror from the faces that are engraven in marble ; and never are to be seen these Western pictures in stone, and statues erected to the immortal memory cf heroes."

. . . . . .

The two Hanoums left for Switzerland.

[1] The answer to such an observation is obvious, but I prefer to present the Hanoum's anecdote as she gave it.—G.E.

# CHAPTER V
## THE ALPS AND ARTIFICIALITY

# CHAPTER V

## THE ALPS AND ARTIFICIALITY

TERRITET, *Dec.* 1906.

I WONDER if you know what life is like in a big *caravanserai* on the shores of Lake Leman in December.   This *hotel* is filled from the ground to the sixth floor, and from east to west with people of all ages, who have a horror of being where they ought to be—that is to say, in their own homes—and who have come to the Swiss mountains with but one idea—that of enjoying themselves.   What can be the matter with their homes, that they are all so anxious to get away ?

I have been more than a month in this place, and cannot get used to it.   After the calm of the Forest of Fontainebleau and the quiet little house where, for the first time, we tasted the joys of real rest, this existence seems to me strange and even unpleasant.   Indeed, it makes me tired even to think of the life these people lead and their expense of muscular force to no purpose.

E

But the doctor wished me to come here, and I, who long above everything else to be strong, am hoping the pure air will cure me.

On the terrace which overlooks the lake I usually take my walks, but when I have taken about a hundred steps I have to sit down and rest.   Certainly I would be no Alpinist.

One thing to which I never seem to accustom myself is my hat.   It is always falling off. Sometimes, too, I forget that I am wearing a hat and lean back in my chair ; and what an absurd fashion—to lunch in a hat !   Still, hats seem to play a very important rôle in Western life. Guess how many I possess at present—twenty.

I cannot tell whom I have to thank, since the parcels come anonymously, but several kind friends, hearing of our escape, have had the thoughtfulness and the same original idea  of providing us with hats.   Hardly a day passes but someone sends us a hat; it is curious, but charming all the same.   Do they think we are too shy to order hats for ourselves, and are still wandering about Switzerland in our *tcharchafs* ? [1]

.        .        .        .        .        .

Every  morning  the  people  here  row  on  the

[1] Tcharchafs = cloak  and  veil  worn  by  Turkish  women when  walking  out  of  doors.

lake, or play tennis—tennis being one of their favourite forms of amusement. I watch them with interest, yet even were I able I should not indulge in this unfeminine sport.

Women rush about the court, from left to right, up and down, forwards and backwards. Their hair is all out of curl, often it comes down; and they wear unbecoming flat shoes and men's shirts and collars and ties.

The ball comes scarcely over the net, a woman rushes forward, her leg is bared to the sight of all; by almost throwing herself on the ground, she hits it back over the net, and then her favourite man (not her husband, I may mention), with whom she waltzes and rows and climbs, chooses this moment to take a snapshot of her most hideous attitude. What an unpleasant idea to think a man should possess such a souvenir!

And yet after tennis these people do not rest— on they go, walking and climbing; and what is the use of it all?—they only come back and eat four persons' share of lunch.

At meal-time, the conversation is tennis and climbing, and climbing and tennis; and again I say, I cannot understand why they employ all this muscular force to no higher end than to give themselves an unnatural appetite.

A friend of my father's, who is staying here, tells me the wonderful climbing he has accomplished.  He explains to me that he has faced death over and over again, and only by the extraordinary pluck of his guide has his life been spared.

" And did you at last reach your friend ? " I asked.

" What friend ? "

" Was it not to rescue some friend that you faced death ? "

" No," he said, " for pleasure."

" For pleasure," I repeated, and he burst out laughing.

He spoke of this as if it were something of which to be proud, " and his oft-repeated encounters with death," he said, " only whetted his appetite for more." Was life then of so little value to this man that he could risk it so easily ?

Naturally in trying to explain this curious existence I compare it with our life in the harem, and the more I think the more am I astonished.  What I should like to ask these people, if I dared, is, are they really satisfied with their lot, or are they only pretending to be

happy, as we in Turkey pretended to be happy ?
Are they not tired of flirting and enjoying themselves so uselessly ?

We in Turkey used to envy the women of the
West. We, who were denied the rights of taking
part in charitable works, imagined that the
European women not only dared to think, but
carry their schemes into action for the betterment of their fellow-creatures.

But are these women here an exception ?
Do they think, or do they not ? I wonder
myself whether they have not found life so
empty that they are endeavouring to crush
out their better selves by using up their physical
energy. How is it possible, I ask myself, that,
after all this exercise, they have strength enough
to dance till midnight. Life to me at present
is all out of focus ; in time perhaps I shall see it
in its proper proportions.

We go down sometimes to see the dancing.
Since I have been here, I perfectly understand
why you never find time to go to balls, if dancing
in your country is anything like it is here. When
we were children of twelve, before we were
veiled, we were invited to dances given in
Constantinople. I have danced with young

attachés at the British Embassy, yet, child
though I was, I saw nothing clever in their
performance.

All the people at this dance are grown up,
not one is under twenty—some are old gentlemen of fifty—yet they romp like children all
through the evening till deep into the night,
using up their energy and killing time, as if
their life depended on the rapidity with which
they hopped round the room without sitting
down or feeling ill.

The waltz is to my mind senseless enough,
but the lancers ?   " The ring of roses " the little
English girls play is more dignified.

It seems to me that women must forfeit a
little of the respect that men owe to them when
they have romped with them at lancers.

To-night, I have found out, dancing here is
after all an excuse for flirting.   In a very short
while couples who were quite unacquainted
with one another become very intimate.   " Oh !
I could not wish for a better death than to die
waltzing," I heard one young woman say to her
partner.   His wishes were the same.   Surely
the air of Switzerland does not engender ambition !

One gentleman came and asked me if I could

A TURKISH DANCER

A TURKISH LADY DRESSED AS A GREEK DANCER

Turkish women spend much of their time dressing up.

dance. I said, " Yes, I can *dance*," laying particular emphasis on the word *dance*. But I do not think he understood.

" Will you dance with me ? " he asked.

" No," I replied, " I *dance* by myself." He stared at me as if I were mad—probably he took me for a professional dancer.

.    .    .    .    .    .

When you come to stay with us at Nice, after we have had enough of this pure air to justify our leaving Switzerland and these commonplace and unsympathetic people, and we are in our own villa again and free to do as we will, then we will teach you Turkish dances, and you will no longer be surprised at my criticisms.

Dancing with us is a fine art. In the Imperial Harem more attention is paid to the teaching of dancing than to any other learning. When the Sultan is worn out with cares of state and the thousand and one other worries for which his autocratic rule is responsible, his dancing girls are called into his presence, and there with veils and graceful movements they soothe his tired nerves till he almost forgets the atrocities which have been committed in his name.

A Turkish woman who dances well is seen to very great advantage ; a dancing woman may become a favourite, a Sultana, a Sultan's mother, the queen of the Imperial Harem.

I can assure you a Western woman is not seen at her best when she dances the lancers. —Your affectionate                ZEYNEB.

# CHAPTER VI

## FREEDOM'S DOUBTFUL ENCHANTMENT

# CHAPTER VI

## FREEDOM'S DOUBTFUL ENCHANTMENT

TERRITET, *Dec.* 1906.

I AM conservative in my habits, as you will find out when you know me better, although Turkish women are generally supposed to be capricious and changeable.

Every day you can picture me sitting on the same terrace, in the same chair, looking at the same reposeful Lake Leman and writing to the same sympathetic friends.

The sea before me is so blue and silent and calm! Does it know, I wonder, the despair which at times fills my soul! or is its blue there to remind me of our home over yonder!

In the spring the Bosphorus had such sweet, sad tints. As children when we walked near its surface my little Turkish friends said to me, "Don't throw stones at the Bosphorus—you will hurt it."

Lake Leman also has ships which destroy the limpid blue of its surface and remind me of those which passed under my lattice windows and sailed so far away that my thoughts could not follow them.

Here I might almost imagine I was looking at the Bosphorus, and yet, is the reflection of snow-clad peaks what I ought to find in the blue sea away yonder? Where are the domes and minarets of our mosques? Is not this the hour when the Muezzins [1] lift up their voices, and solemnly call the faithful to prayer?

On such an autumn evening as this in Stamboul, I should be walking in a quiet garden where chrysanthemums would be growing in profusion. The garden would be surrounded by high walls, giant trees would throw around us a damp and refreshing shade, and the red rays of the dying sun would find their way through the leaves, and my companions' white dresses would all be stained with its roseate hues.

But suddenly we remember the sun is setting. To the cries of the frightened birds we hurry back quickly through the trees. How can a

---

[1] Muezzins = the religious teachers amongst the Mohammedans, whose duty it is five times a day to ascend the minaret and call the faithful followers of Mohammed to prayer from the four corners of the earth.

Turkish woman dare to be out after sunset ? . . .
Ah ! I see it all again now—those garden walls,
those knotted trees, those jealous lattice-work
windows which give it all an impression of dis-
tress ! and I am looking at it without a veil
and eyes that are free !

.       .       .       .       .       .

Even as I write to you, young men and
maidens pass and repass before me, and I
wonder more than ever whether they are happy
—yet what do they know of life and all its
sorrows ; sorrow belongs to the Turks—they
have bought its exclusive rights.

In spite of our efforts not to have ourselves
spoken about, the Sultan still interests himself
in us. In all probability, he has had us reported as " dangerous revolutionists " whom
the Swiss Government would do well to watch.
And perhaps the Swiss authorities, having had
so many disagreeable experiences of anarchists
of late, are keeping their eyes on us ! Yet why
should we care ? All our lives have we not been
thus situated ? We ought to be used to it by this
time.

Around me I see people breathing in the pure
air, going out and coming in, and no government watches their movements. Why should

*Fate* have chosen certain persons rather than others to place under such intolerable conditions ?   Why should we have been born Turks rather than these free women who are here enjoying life ?   I ask myself this question again and again, and all to no purpose; it only makes me bitter.

Do you know, I begin to regret that I ever came in contact with your Western education and culture !   But if I begin writing of Western culture, this letter will not be finished for weeks, and I want news of you very soon.—Au revoir, petite chérie,                          ZEYNEB.

.     .     .     .     .     .

TERRITET, *Jan.* 1907.

Your letter of yesterday annoys me.   You are " changing your *pension*," you say, " because you are not free to come in to meals when you like."

What an awful grievance !   If only you English women knew how you are to be envied ! Come, follow me to Turkey, and I will make you thank Allah for your liberty.

Ever since I can remember, I have had a passion for writing, but this is rather the exception than the rule for a Turkish woman.   At

one time of my life, I exchanged picture post-
cards with unknown correspondents, who sent
me, to a *poste restante* address, views of places
and people I hoped some day to visit.

This correspondence was for us the DREAM
SIDE of our existence. In times of unhappiness
(extra unhappiness, for we were always unhappy),
discouragement, and, above all, revolt, it was in
this existence that we tried to find refuge. The
idea that friends were thinking of us, however
unknown they were, made us look upon life with
a little more resignation—and you, my friend,
who complain that " you are not free to have
your meals when you like," should know that
*this correspondence had to be hidden with as much
care, as if it had been a plot to kill the Imperial
Majesty himself.*

.      .      .      .      .      .

When our correspondence was sent to us
direct, it had to pass through the hands of three
different persons before we had the pleasure of
receiving it ourselves. All the letters we sent
out and received were read not only by my
father and his secretary, but by the officials
of the Ottoman Post.

One day, I remember, the daughter of an
ex-American minister sent me a long account

of her sister's marriage, and she stopped short at the fourth page. I was just going to write to her for an explanation, when the remaining sheets were sent on to me by the police, whose duty it was to read the letters, and who had simply forgotten to put the sheets in with the others.

You could never imagine the plotting and intriguing necessary to receive the most ordinary letters; not even the simplest action could be done in a straightforward manner; we had to perjure our souls by constantly pretending, in order to enjoy the most innocent pleasures—it mattered little to us, I do assure you, " whether we had our meals at the time we liked " or not.

.    .    .    .    .    .

All around me little girls are playing. They wear their hair loose or in long plaits, their dresses are short. Up the steps they climb; they play at hide-and-seek with their brothers and their brothers' friends. They laugh, they romp, their eyes are full of joy, and their complexions are fresh—surely this is the life children should lead ?

I close my eyes, and I see the children of my own country who at their age are veiled. Their childhood has passed before they know it. They do not experience the delight of playing in the sun, and when they go out they wear thick black veils which separate them from all the joys of youth.

I was scarcely ten years old when I saw one of my little friends taking the veil, and from that day she could no longer play with us. That incident created such an impression on us that for days we could hardly speak. Poor little Suate! No longer could she dance with us at the Christians' balls nor go to the circus. Her life had nothing more in common with ours, and we cried for her as if she had died.

But we were happy not to be in her place, and I remember saying to my sister, " Well, at least I have two years before me; perhaps in a short time our customs will have changed. What is the use of worrying so long beforehand ? "

" I am still more certain to escape, for I have four years before me," she answered.

Little Suate was veiled at a time when those delightful volumes of the *Bibliothèque Rose* were almost part of our lives. From them we learnt to believe that some good fairy must come, and with the touch of her magic wand all our destinies would be changed.

But to-day, when I am no longer a child, I ask

F

myself whether my great-great-grandchildren can ever free themselves from this hideous bondage.

Melek is writing for you her impressions of taking the veil. They are more recent than mine.—Your affectionate        ZEYNEB.

# CHAPTER VII

## GOOD-BYE TO YOUTH — TAKING THE VEIL

# CHAPTER VII

## GOOD-BYE TO YOUTH — TAKING THE VEIL

TERRITET, *Jan.* 1907.

I AM thinking of a sad spring morning of long ago. I was twelve years old, but the constant terror in which I had lived had increased my tendency towards uneasiness and melancholy. The life I was forced to lead had nothing in common with my nature. Ever since I can remember, I had loved the bright light, open horizons, galloping on horses against the wind, and all my surroundings were calm and monotonous.

As time went on, I put off every day the moment for wakening, because I had to open my eyes in the same room, and the same white muslin curtains were always there to greet me.

How can I explain to you my jealousy at seeing how contentedly all the furniture lay in the soft light which filtered through the latticed windows of our harems ? A heavy weight was pressing on my spirit ! How many times when the governess came into my room did she not find me in tears !

" What is the matter, my darling ? " she would ask, and under the influence of this unexpected tenderness I would sob without even knowing the cause of my sorrow.

Then I dressed myself slowly, so that there should be less time to live. How was it, I wondered, that some people feared death ? Death would have been such a change—the only change to which a Turkish woman could look forward.

In our house there was scarcely a sound ; hardly were the steps of the young Circassian slaves heard as they passed along the corridors.

Our mother was kind but stern, and her beautiful face had an expression of calm resignation. She lived like a stranger amongst us, not being able to associate herself with either our thoughts or our ideals.

The schoolroom where we worked the greater part of the day looked on to a garden thick with trees and perfumed with the early roses. Its furniture consisted of a big oak table and chairs, shelves full of books, a globe, and three busts in plaster of Paris, of Napoleon, Dante, and

Mozart. What strange thoughts have those three men, so different and yet so interesting, not suggested to me ! What a curious influence they all three had on my child mind !

It was in this schoolroom, twice a week, that we studied the Koran; but before the lesson began an old servant covered up the three great men in plaster. The *Hodja* [1] must not see these heathenish figures.

When the Imam arrived, my sister and I went to the door to meet him, kissing his hand as a sign of respect. Then he used to pass his bony fingers over our hair, saying as a greeting, " May Allah protect you, my children."

With the Hodja Effendi came into our schoolroom a perfume of incense of burnt henna and sandal-wood. His green tunic and turban, which showed he had visited the Holy Tomb at Mecca, made his beard so white and his eyes so pale, that he seemed like a person from another world—indeed he reminded me, not a little, of those Indian Fakirs, who live on prayers.

From the moment he sat down at the table, my sorrows seemed to vanish for a while, and an atmosphere of calm and blessed peace took possession of my soul.

[1] Hodja = teacher of the Koran.

" Only God is God," he began.

" And Mahomet is His Prophet," we responded, as we opened the Koran at the place he had chosen for the lesson.

" Read, my child," he said.

I took the book, and began to read the prayer, which is a rhythmed chant. The Imam read with me in a soft, low voice, and when the chapter was finished he murmured, " You read well, Neyr ; may Allah protect you."

Then he questioned us on the prayers we had learnt, on the good we had to do and the evil to avoid, and his voice was so monotonous that each sentence sounded like a prayer.

When we had finished, he asked, as he always did, to see our governess. I went to find her in the garden, and she came at once.

As the Hodja could not speak English, he asked us to say to her, " You have a fine face. Allah loves the good and the kind and those who go the way they should go. He will be with you." And before he went away, taking with him the delightful perfume of incense, he shook the hand of the Englishwoman in his.

Another day he came, and after the lesson he said to me, " Neyr, you are twelve years old ; you must be veiled. You can no longer have

TURKISH LADY IN TCHARCHAFF.  OUTDOOR COSTUME

During the reign of Abdul Aziz (*vide* text) Turkish ladies wore the Yashmak in the street, now they wear a thick black veil through which they can see and are not supposed to be seen.  The women must always wear gloves.

your hair exposed and your face uncovered—
you must be veiled. Your mother has not
noticed you have grown a big girl, I therefore
must. I teach you to love Allah, you are my
spiritual child, and for that reason I must warn
you of the danger henceforward of going out
unveiled. Neyr, you must be veiled."

I was not even listening to the Imam! An
awful agony had seized and numbed my soul;
the words which he had uttered resounded in
my brain, and little by little sank into my understanding—" Neyr, you must be veiled "—
that is to say, to be forever cloistered like those
who live around you ; to be a slave like your
mother, and your cousins, and your elder sister;
to belong henceforth to the harem ; no longer
to play in the garden unveiled ; nor ride Arabian
ponies in the country ; to have a veil over your
eyes, and your soul ; to be always silent, always
forgotten, to be always and always *a thing*.

" Neyr, you must be veiled," the old Hodja
began again.

I raised my head. " Yes, I know, Hodja
Effendi, I shall be veiled, since it is necessary."
Then I was silent.

The old Imam went away, not understanding
what had happened to me, and without my

having kissed his hand. I remained in the same place, my elbows on the table. I was alone. All around was deadly still.

Suddenly, however, Miss M. opened the door; her eyes were red. Gently shutting the door and coming towards me, she said :

" Neyr, I have seen the Imam, and I understand that from to-morrow you must be veiled."

I saw the pain stamped on her face, but I could say nothing. Already she had taken me in her arms and carried me into her room at the end of the corridor, murmuring all the while, " The brutes ! "

Together we wept ; I, without unnecessary complaints, she without useless consolation.

Once my sorrow had passed a little, I questioned my governess.

" You are English, are you not ? "

" Yes, dear, I am English."

" In England are the women veiled, and the children free ? "

" The women and children are free."

" Then I will go to England."

" Silence, Neyr, silence."

" Take me to England."

" I cannot, Neyr," she answered.

But all that day and all that night I dreamt of dear, free England, I longed to see.

. . . . . .

The country house where we lived was large, with big rooms, long corridors, and dark halls. Now and again carriages passed, bringing excursionists to the neighbouring wood, and when we heard the wheels rumbling over the uneven road, we rushed to the latticed windows to see all we could.

Sometimes we used to go with Miss M. to see Stamboul, which was on the opposite shore. Miss M. loved the town, and used to take us there as often as possible. Sometimes we used to ride with my brother in the country, and I loved to feel the wind blowing through my untidy hair, but all that would be over now. Sometimes my father would take me to see friends of his—foreigners they were—and the girls and boys played together, and I laughed and played with them. But I understood that I was only on the margin of their great life, that each day part of my right to existence would be taken from me, a veil would soon cover my face, and I would only be a Moslem woman, whose every aspiration and emotion would be trampled under foot.

That moment had come.

.     .     .     .     .     .

We were to go out with mother that afternoon. On my bed in the monotonous room I disliked so much, a black mantle, a cape, and a veil were placed.

Several persons had come to see me veiled for the first time. Awkwardly I placed the pleated skirt round my waist, the cape over my shoulders, and the veil over my face; but, in order that the tears which were falling should not be seen, I did not lift it up again.

" Neyr," asked mother, " are you ready ? "

" Yes," I answered, and followed her with my head up in spite of this mourning. And from that day, from that moment, I had determined on revolt.

MELEK (N. NEYR-EL-NIRSA).

# CHAPTER VIII

## A MISFIT EDUCATION

# CHAPTER VIII

## A MISFIT EDUCATION

Territet, *Jan.* 1907.

I BEGAN to write to you the other day of the influence which Western culture has had on the lives of Turkish women.

If you only knew the disastrous consequences of that learning and the suffering for which it is responsible ! From complete ignorance, we were plunged into the most advanced culture ; there was no middle course, no preparatory school, and, indeed, what ought to have been accomplished in centuries we have done in three, and sometimes in two generations.

When our grandmothers could sign their names and read the Koran, they were known as " cultured women " compared with those who had never learnt to read and write ; when a woman could dispense with the services of a " public letter-writer " she was looked upon as a learned woman in the town in which she lived, and her time was fully occupied writing the correspondence of her neighbours.

What I call the disastrous influence was the influence of the Second French Empire.

One day, when I have time, I shall look up the papers which give a description of the Empress Eugénie's visit to the East. No doubt they will treat her journey as a simple exchange of courtesies between two Sovereigns. They may lay particular emphasis on the pageantry of her reception, but few women of that time were aware of the revolution that this visit had on the lives of the Turkish women.

The Empress of the French was incontestably beautiful—but *she was a woman*, and the first impression which engraved itself on the understanding of these poor Turkish captives, was, that their master, Abdul Aziz, was paying homage *to a woman*.

The extraordinary beauty and charm of the Empress was enhanced by the most magnificent reception ever offered to a Sovereign, and even to-day, one figure stands out from all that wonderful Oriental pageant—a slight, lovely woman before whom a Sultan bowed in all his majesty.

In honour of a *woman*, a jewelled palace in marble and gold was being built, and from the opposite side of the Bosphorus the captives watched it coming into existence with ever-increasing wonderment.

For a *woman*, had been prepared rose and gold caïques all carpeted with purple velvet. From a magnificent little Arabian kiosk especially built Ottoman troops from all corners of the Empire passed in review before a *woman*; even her bath sandals were all studded with priceless gems ; no honour was too high, no luxury too great for *this woman*. The Sultanas could think of nothing else ; in the land of Islam great honour had been rendered to a *woman*.

It was after the visit of the Empress Eugénie that the women of the palace and the wives of the high functionaries copied as nearly as they could the appearance of the beautiful Empress. They divided their hair in the middle, and spent hours in making little bunches of curls. High-heeled shoes replaced the coloured *babouches* ; [1] they even adopted the hideous crinolines, and abandoned forever those charming Oriental

---

[1] Babouche = Turkish slippers without heels.

garments, the *chalvar*[1] and *enturi*,[2] which they considered symbols of servitude, but which no other fashion has been able to equal in beauty.

As might be supposed, the middle class soon followed the example of the palace ladies and adopted Western costume. Then there was a craze for *everything* French. The most eccentric head-dresses and daring costumes were copied. To these Oriental women were given more jewels than liberty, more sensual love than pure affection, and it mattered little, until they found out from reading the foreign papers that there was something else except the beauty of the body —the beauty of the soul.

The more they read and learnt, the greater was their suffering. They read everything they could lay their hands on—history, religion, philosophy, poetry, and even *risqué* books. They had an indigestion of reading, and no one was there to cure them.

This desire for everything French lasted until our generation. No one seemed to understand

[1] Chalvar = Turkish pantaloons, far more graceful than the hideous harem skirts, which met with such scant success in this country.

[2] Enturi = the tunic, heavily embroidered, which almost covered the pantaloons.

how harmful it was to exaggerate the atmosphere of excitement in which we were living.

With the craze for the education of the West, French governesses came to Constantinople in great numbers ; for it was soon known what high salaries the Turks paid, and how hospitable they were.

If you had seen the list of books that these unfortunate Turkish girls read to get a knowledge of French literature, I think you would agree with me they must have been endowed with double moral purity for the books not to have done them more harm.

For nearly thirty years this dangerous experiment went on. No parents seemed to see the grave error of having in one's house a woman about whom they knew nothing, and who in a very short time could exert a very disastrous influence over a young life. It was only when catastrophe after catastrophe [1] had brought

[1] The Western governesses, in so many cases, took no interest in their pupils' reading, and allowed them to read everything they could lay their hands on. With their capacity for intrigue, they smuggled in principally French novels of the most harmful kind. Physical exercise being impossible to work off the evil effects of this harmful reading, the Turkish woman, discontented with her lot, saw only two ways of ending her unhappy existence—flight or suicide ; she generally preferred the latter method.

this to their notice, they began to take any
interest in their daughters' governesses, and
occupy themselves a little more seriously about
what they read.

When I look back on our girlhood, I do feel
bitterly towards these women, who had not the
honesty to find out that we had souls.  How
they might have helped us if only they had
cared !  How they might have discussed with us
certain theories which we were trying to apply
disastrously to our Eastern existence !  But
they said to themselves, no doubt, Let us take
advantage of the high salary, for we cannot
stand this tedious existence too long.  And the
Turkish women went on reading anything that
came within their reach.

Could these Turkish girls be blamed for thus
unknowingly destroying their own happiness ?
What was there to do but read ?  When all
the recognised methods of enjoyment are re-
moved, and when few visits are paid (and to go
out every day is not considered ladylike), think
what an enormous part of the day is still left
unoccupied.

In our grandmothers' days, the women used
to assemble in the evening and make those

beautiful embroideries which you admire so much.  Others made their daughters' trousseaux, others told stories in the Arabian Nights style, and with that existence they were content. Not one of them wanted to read the fashionable French novels, nor had they any desire to play the piano.

It was at the beginning of the reign of Abdul Hamid that this craze for Western culture was at its height.  The terrible war, and the fall of the two beloved Sultans, woke the women from their dreams.  Before the fact that their country was in danger, they understood their duty. From odalisques [1] they became mothers and wives determined to give their children the education they themselves had so badly needed.

The new monarch then endowed the Ottoman Empire with schools for little girls.  The pupils who applied themselves learnt very quickly, and soon they could favourably be compared with their sisters of the West.

This was the first step that Turkish women had made towards their evolution.

.    .    .    .    .    .

At the age of ten, when I began the study of

[1] Slaves.

English, we were learning at the same time French, Arabic, and Persian, as well as Turkish. Not one of these languages is easy, but no one complained, and every educated Turkish girl had to undergo the same torture.

What I disliked most bitterly in my school days was the awful regularity. My mother, rather the exception than the rule, found we must be always occupied. As a child of twelve, I sat almost whole days at the piano, and when I was exhausted, Mdlle. X. was told to give me needlework. Delighted to be rid of me, she gave me slippers to work for my father, whilst she wrote to "Mon cher Henri." She took no notice of me, as I stitched away, sighing all the while. In order to get finished quickly, I applied myself to my task ; the more I hurried, the more I was given to do, and in a few weeks the drawers were full of my work. Our education was overdone.

.     .     .     .     .     .

So we Turkish women came to a period of our existence when it was useless to sigh for a mind that could content itself with the embroidery evenings of our grandmothers. These gatherings, too, became less and less frequent, for

"SILENT GOSSIP" OF A GROUP OF TURKISH WOMEN

They will often spend an afternoon in silent communion.

TURKISH LADIES IN THEIR GARDEN WITH THEIR CHILDREN'S GOVERNESSES

Little boys remain in the Harem until they are eight, after that they are
counted as men.

women were not allowed out after dark, no matter what their age.

Then it was, however, that, in spite of its being forbidden, I inaugurated a series of " white dinner parties "[1] for girls only. This created a scandal throughout the town. Our parents disliked the idea intensely, but we remained firm, and were happy to see our efforts crowned with success. Later, when we were married, we continued those dinners as long as we dared, and then it was we discussed what we could do for the future of women.

And what delightful evenings we spent together! Those *soirées* were moments when we could be ourselves, open our hearts to one another, and try to brighten for a little our lives. The fourteen friends I most loved in Turkey were all of the company of " white diners," and all those fourteen girls have played some special rôle in life.

. . . . . .

I am sending you a letter, written by a friend whom I shall never see again.

[1] They were called " white " because they were originally attended by unmarried women only, and they all wore white dresses.—G. E.

" Since your departure," she wrote, " we have not been allowed to go a step out of doors, lest we should follow your example. We are living under a régime of terror which is worse than it has ever been before.

" I want to implore you to work for us. Tell the whole world what we are suffering ; indeed it would be a consolation, much as it hurts our pride."

.    .    .    .    .    .

I look around me and see all these happy children here in Switzerland without one care, and again I say to myself, how unjust is life. —Your affectionate friend,    ZEYNEB.

# CHAPTER IX
## "SMART WOMEN" THROUGH THE VEIL

# CHAPTER IX

## "SMART WOMEN" THROUGH THE VEIL

IN answer to my query as to whether Caux had smart enough visitors to justify an editor sending there a special correspondent, I had the following letter from Zeyneb :

CAUX, Jan. 1907.

The articles which I have written for you on the beauties of Switzerland will possibly not appeal to the British public.

For a long time last night, when I returned to my room, I tried to make you understand the intense delight I had felt in watching the good-night kiss which the lovesick moon had given to the beautiful lake, before going away far into space.

This moon scene reminds me more than ever of one of our magnificent moonlights on the Bosphorus, and I am sure if you had been with me on the Terrace you would have loved the

moonlit Bosphorus for its resemblance to Leman,
and Leman for helping you to understand how
wonderful is the Bosphorus.   But the poetry of
moonlight does not appeal evidently to the
British soul, since they are clamouring for news
of people who are " smart."

I have always wondered at the eagerness with
which the society ladies here seize the paper.
Now I understand—it is to see whether their
names are included amongst people " who are
smart."   What a morbid taste, to want to see
one's name in a newspaper !

I could not tell you whether the people or
the life at Caux would be considered smart.
They certainly are extraordinary, and the life
they lead seems to me to be a complete reversal
of all prevailing customs.   From early in the
morning till late at night they toboggan and
skate.   Everything is arranged with a view to
the practice of these two sports.   I cannot tell
you the disagreeable impression that the women
produce on me, sitting astride of their little
machines and coming down the slope with a
giddy rapidity.   Their hair is all out of order,
their faces vivid scarlet, and their skirts, arranged
like those of a Cambodgian dancer, are lacking

in grace. But this is not a competition for a beauty prize; all that counts is to go more quickly down the course than the others, no matter whether you kill yourself in the attempt.

That there are people in England who are interested in knowing who is staying at a Swiss Hotel, the guests they receive, and the clothes they wear, is an unpleasant discovery for me. I thought English people were more intelligent.

One of the reasons for which we left Turkey was, that we could no longer bear the degrading supervision of the Sultan's spies. But is it not almost the same here ? Here, too, there are detectives of a kind ! Alas ! Alas ! there is no privacy inside or outside Turkey.

The people who interest me most are not the smart ladies, but the Swiss themselves. They alone in all this cosmopolitan crowd know that the sun has flooded with its golden tints the wonderful panorama of their mountains, the lake stretches out in a mystery of mauve and rose, and they alone have time to bow in admiration to the Creator of Beauty and the great Poet of Nature.—Affectionately,

ZEYNEB.

# CHAPTER X

## THE TRUE DEMOCRACY

# CHAPTER X

## THE TRUE DEMOCRACY—THE IMPOSSIBILITY OF SNOBBERY IN TURKISH LIFE

THE two fugitives left Switzerland for Nice. Melek was in perfect health, and still delighted with her Western liberty.

Zeyneb, although better, began more and more to see her new life lose its glamour. But it was too late—there was no going back.

I wonder which of the two suffers more—the person who expects much and is disappointed; or the person of whom much is expected and feels she has disappointed. It seemed to me so often, I could often read in Zeyneb's eyes, " Was it worth it ? " Was she like the woman of her own country, counting the cost when the debt had already been incurred. I, who thought I saw this, suffered in consequence.

Perhaps, as elder sister and ringleader in the preparations for their flight, Zeyneb was feeling her responsibility. Would the younger sister, when the glamour of freedom had passed, reproach her for the step they had taken ? That was a question that had to be left to the uncertain answer of the Future.

A little while after they were installed at Nice, Zeyneb resumed her correspondence with me.

NICE, 15th Feb. 1907.

For a week now we have had the sun shining almost as in the East. After the mountains and the snow of Switzerland, how good it is to be here ! I just love to watch the blue sky, the flowers and the summer dresses ! And I am warm again for a little while.

We are living at Cimiez, well up the hill, in a little villa surrounded by a big garden full of flowers and exotic plants and a few cypress trees; the only sad note in our whole surroundings, except for us its name, the Villa Selma, for curiously enough our villa has a Turkish name—the name of a friend for whom the sadness of life had been too great, and who is now sleeping under the shade of the cypress in a *comfortable cemetery* [1] in our own land. How

---

[1] It sounds strange to the Western mind to speak of a "comfortable cemetery," but the dead are very near to the

strange that fate should have directed our steps to a villa that bears her name, and surrounded us with trees that remind us day and night of her past existence.

Hardly had we arrived at Nice, when in a restaurant we met a lady friend from Turkey, a friend whom the Sultan, in a fit of madness, or shall I call it prudence, allowed to come to Nice with her husband and children for a change of air. Our departure, no doubt, has made this great despot think, and in order to prove to all his subjects how great was his generosity, he had allowed this woman to travel alone as she wished.

But we did not waste time discussing the psychology of Hamid's character, we were only too delighted to see one another. How many things had we not to talk about! how many impressions had we not in common! If only a snapshot had been taken of us and sent to Constantinople what a very bad impression it would have made on our poor captive friends away yonder. How they would have envied us!

living Turks; the cemetery is the Turkish woman's favourite walk, and the greatest care is taken of the last resting-place of the loved ones.—G. E.

Imagine ! the next day we all three lunched together at Monte Carlo, and that *without our friend's husband !* We were seated on the terrace overlooking the blue sea, and the new-comer was breathing in the " free air " for the first time, whilst we, old refugees of a year, were pleased to see her enthusiasm.

" When I think," she said, " that only three of us are enjoying this liberty compared to the thousands of poor women who have not any idea of what they have been deprived, it makes me unhappy."

But the weather was too fine for such sad thoughts. Near us a Hungarian band was play-ing, and it seemed so in harmony with the sur-roundings. Not one of the faces round us betrayed the least suspicion of sadness. Could they all be happy, these unknown people ? It really matters so little—we are happy as prisoners to whom liberty has been given, and it is at a moment like this that we appreciate it most.

At dessert, after having discussed many ques-tions, we finally spoke of the dear country which only she of us three would see again, and now, a certain melancholy overshadows the table where a while ago we were so gay.

The Orient is like a beautiful poem which is always sad, even its very joy is sadness. All Eastern stories end in tragedy. Even the landscape which attracts by its beauty has its note of sorrow, and yet one of the many women writers who was introduced to us, and welcomed as our guest, said to me : " I never laughed anywhere as I laughed in Constantinople." That was quite true, for I was witness of her delightful merriment, always caught from one of us ; for no one can laugh like a Turkish woman when she takes the trouble.

The foundation of our character is joyous, persistently joyous, since neither the monotony of our existence, nor the tragedy of the Hamidian régime, nor the lamentable circumstances of our life has been able to utterly crush laughter out of life. There is no middle course in Turkey.

But I told you that it was from studying the customs of Western Europe that I was beginning to better understand the land I had left. If the joys of freedom have been denied to Turkish women, how many worries have they been spared. Are not women to be sincerely pitied who make " Society " the aim and object of their existence ? No longer can they do what they feel they ought for fear of compromising a "social position." Is not the *gaiety* of their lives worse even than the *monotony* of ours? Ofttimes they have to sacrifice a noble friendship to the higher demands of social exclusiveness. How strange and narrow and insincere it all seems to a Turkish woman.

I never made the acquaintance of the disease "snobbery" in my own land. Here, for the first time, I have an opportunity of studying its victims. There may be something wanting in my Turkish constitution to prevent my appreciating the rare delight of a visit from a great *personage.* Ambitious people I have often met —in what country do they not thrive? There are many in Turkey, and that is only natural when it is remembered the very limited number of ways for individuality to express itself. But snobs! How childish they are! Can they really believe I am a more desirable person to have at a tea-table since I have been noticed by an ex-Empress? Only by inflicting their society on people who obviously do not want them, and by "bluff"—another word which does not exist in the Turkish language—can they be invited at all. Not a single woman in

the whole of Turkey would put so low an esti-
mate on her own importance! So snobbery
would never get a foothold with us.

You cannot know how this simple black veil,
which covers our faces, can completely change
the whole conditions of the life of a nation.

What is there in common between you and us ?

" The heart," you will say.

But is the heart the same in the East as in
the West ? And what a difference there is
between our method of seeing things, even of
great importance. Ambition with us does not
seek the same ends; pride with us is wounded
by such a different class of actions; and individuality in the East seeks other gratifications
than it does in the West.

How would it be possible for " snobbery " to
exist in a country where there is no society,
and where the ideal of democracy is so admir-
ably understood; where the poor do not envy
the rich, the servant respects his master, and
the humble do not crave for the position of
Grand Vizier ?

I said there were ambitious people in my
country, yes; but they are still more fatalists.
If a man has been unsuccessful, he blames his

" written destiny," which no earthly being can
alter.   Is not this resignation to the yoke of
the tyrannical Sultan a proof of fatalism ?
What other nation would, for thirty-one years,
have put up with such a régime ?

It is only since I have seen other Governments and other peoples that I can fully realise
the passionate fatalism of the Turks.

Those " discontents," whom I knew, were the
true " Believers," for at least they knew how
to distinguish between belief and useless resignation.   Their number, fortunately, grows every
day.   More and more impatiently am I waiting
for the result of a Revolution intelligently
arranged, the aim of which will be the Liberty
of the Individual, and the uplifting of the race.

.        .        .        .        .        .

And yet a *revoltée* though I was, I think I
envied my grandmother's calm happiness.

" My poor little girls," she used to say, " your
young days are so much sadder than mine.   At
your age I didn't think of changing the face of
the world, nor working for the betterment of
the human race, still less for raising the status
of women.   Our mothers taught us the Koran,
and we had confidence in its laws.   If one of

us had less happiness than another, we never thought of revolting; 'it was written,' we said, and we had not the presumption to try to change our destiny."

" Grandmother," I asked her, " is it our fault if we are unhappy ? We have read so many books which have shown us the ugly side of our life in comparison with the lives of the women of the West. We are young. We long for just a little joy; and, grandmother," I added slowly, and with emphasis, " we want to be free, to find it ourselves."

Did she understand ? That I cannot tell, for she did not answer, but her eyes were fixed on us in unending sadness ; then suddenly she dropped them again on to her embroidery.

In the autumn or in the spring our darling grandmother came to fetch us to stay with her in her lovely home at Smyrna. I must add, to point out to you another beautiful feature of our Turkish life, that this woman was not my father's own mother. She was my late grandfather's seventh and only living widow, but she treated all my grandfather's children with equal tenderness. Rarely is it otherwise in Turkey. She loved us, this dear, dear woman, quite as much, if not more, than the children of her own daughter, and we never supposed till we came to the West there was anything exceptional in this attachment. Just as a woman loves her own children, she cares for the children of a former wife, confident, when her time comes to die, her children will be well treated by her successor.

In our grandmother's home life was just a lovely long dream ; a life of peace unceasing— the life of a Turkish woman before the régime of Hamid and thoughts of Revolution haunted our existence. Every evening young women and girls brought musical instruments. First, there was singing, then one after another we danced, and the one who danced the best was applauded and made to dance until she almost fell exhausted.

Towards midnight we supped by the light of the moon, either in our garden or at friends' houses ; and we talked and danced and laughed, all so happy in one another's society, and none of us remembering we were subjects of a Mighty Tyrant, who, had we been at Constantinople, would have stopped those festivities by order of the police.

The gatherings in this house, covered with wisteria and roses, and surrounded by an old-world garden, where flowers were allowed to grow with a liberty of which we were jealous, were moments of joy indescribable. It was good for us to be in a garden not trimmed and pruned and spoilt as are the gardens of the West, but whose greatest charm is that it can be its own dear natural self; to live in peace when the meaning of terror had been learnt, and comparative freedom when we had known captivity.

If ever you have a chance find out for yourself the difference between the harems in the town and those of the country, then I know you will understand the few really happy moments of my life.—Your affectionate friend

ZEYNEB.

# CHAPTER XI

## A COUNTRY PICTURE

# CHAPTER XI

## A COUNTRY PICTURE

SOMETIMES in the summer afternoons, in large parties, and in big springless waggons, we drove to the olive woods or the vineyards near the seashore. In spite of our veils, we just revelled in the beauty of the sky and the scenery all round. Sometimes we spent all day in the country, lunching on the grass, and playing like children, happy, though not free. Then we went for excursions—wonderful excursions to the ruins of Ephesus and Hierapolis and Parganu. Those women who had learnt Ancient History explained the ruins to the others, and all that mass of crumbling stones took life and breath for us captives.

Many times, too, we stayed with the country people, who divided up their rooms for us, and we lived their life for a time. Those were the moments when I learnt to know and appreciate our fine, trustworthy, primitive Turks. With what kindness they took care of us, paying particular attention to our beds, our meals, our horses, even our attendant eunuchs! Whole families put themselves at our disposal, and very often they would not let us pay for anything we had had during our stay. In no country in the world, I am sure, could such hospitality and such cordial generosity be found, being as we were to them perfect strangers.

One day at Gondjeli, after having visited the ruins of Taacheer, we lost the last train home. One of our attendants, however, called on the Imam, who was known throughout the village for his kindness. He and his wife, a delightful woman whom I shall never forget, not only gave us food and lodging for the night, but the next day begged us to stay longer.

We were five women and three attendants. The meals offered us were abundant; the beds, simple mattresses thrown on the floor, were spotlessly clean, and ever so daintily arranged; and the next morning, early, before we dressed, our baths were ready. When the moment of departure came mother wished to leave them something for all the trouble they had taken. But the old Imam answered : "My child, there are no poor in our village. Each man here has his own little bit of ground to till, and enough bread to eat. Why should he ask Allah for more ? "

I have often thought of those words. Every time I used to look at the useless luxury of our Turkish households, the Imam's little modest dwelling and his kindly face rose up to reproach me.—Your affectionate  ZEYNEB.

I

# CHAPTER XII

## THE STAR FROM THE WEST—THE EMPRESS EUGÉNIE

# CHAPTER XII

## THE STAR FROM THE WEST—THE EMPRESS EUGÉNIE

NICE, *Feb.* 1907.

WE have just returned from Cap Martin, where we have had the pleasure and honour of being introduced to the Empress Eugénie, the person of all persons I hoped to meet in Europe. Never will she know how much I have appreciated seeing her to-day, and all the charming past she called back to my memory.

Imagine actually seeing in the flesh, the heroine of your grandmothers' stories; the Empress whose beauty fascinated the East, the Empress whose clothes the women copied, whose language they learnt, the woman who had, though perhaps she may not know it, the greatest influence on the lives of Turkish women. It seemed to me as I looked at the ex-Empress, that I was back in Constantinople again, but the Constantinople that my grandmother had

133

known, the Constantinople where the Sultan Abdul-Aziz reigned and the life of the Turkish women was one of independence compared to ours.

The Empress remembered with great pleasure every detail of her visit to the East. She spoke of the persons she had known, and asked for news of them. Alas! so many were dead, and others scattered to the four corners of the Empire!

She remembered the town, the Palaces, and the marble Beylerbei which had been built specially for her. So kindly, too, did she speak of the Sultan Aziz, saying how welcome he had made her, and how his people loved him.

Was it possible without appearing unpatriotic to make her understand that the lovely Palace in which she had stayed, the Palace which had echoed with the sounds of Eastern music and dancing and singing, was now being put to a very different usage? During Hamid's reign Palaces are not required for festivity, but captivity. Many unfortunate souls have only known Beylerbei as the stepping stone to Eternity!

I should have liked to remind the Empress, had I dared, of the impression her beauty had made on the women.

Yashmak and Mantle (Feradjé)

She is an old lady now, but she did not seem so to me. I was looking at the Empress my countrywomen had admired, the Empress for whom they had sacrificed their wonderful Eastern garments; I saw the curls they had copied, the little high-heeled shoes she wore, and even the jewels she had liked best.

" Are the women still as much veiled as when I was in Constantinople?" asked the Empress; and when I told her that a thick black veil had taken the place of the white Yachmack, she could hardly believe it. "What a pity!" she said, " it was so pretty."

The home in which I saw the Empress, reminded me of one of our Turkish Islands. The sea was as blue and the sky as clear, and the sun, which forced her to change her place several times, was almost as intense. With an odour of pine wood was mixed a fragrant perfume of violets, and the more I looked at it, the more Oriental did the landscape become.

Having spoken so much about the past and the people and the country we have left for ever, it seemed to me that all of us had given way to the inevitable Oriental sadness, yet we fought against it, for there were other visitors there.

I shall always regret not having had the opportunity of seeing the Empress alone; it seemed to me that so much of what I might have told her had been left unsaid, and I know she would have been so glad to listen.—Your affectionate ZEYNEB.

# CHAPTER XIII

## TURKISH HOSPITALITY—A REVOLUTION
## FOR CHILDREN

# CHAPTER XIII

## TURKISH HOSPITALITY—A REVOLUTION FOR CHILDREN

NICE, *March* 1907.

I CAN assure you, I do not exaggerate our Oriental hospitality. Go to Turkey and you will see for yourself that everywhere you will be received like a Queen. Everyone will want to be honoured by your presence in their home.

The most modest household has its rooms for the *mussafirs* or guests. In wealthy establishments, the guest is given the choicest furniture, the daintiest golden goblets and bon-bon dishes, the best and finest linen and embroideries, a little trousseau for her own use, and slaves in constant attendance.

I never remember sitting down to a meal without guests being present. All our rooms for the *mussafirs* were filled, and in this matter my family was by no means the exception;

everyone received with the same pleasure. In England, I believe, you do have guest-rooms, but here in France they do not understand the elements of hospitality.

You cannot imagine how it shocked me when I first heard a French son paid his father for board, and that here in France for a meal received, a meal must be returned. Surely this is not the case in England ?

Often have I tried to find a satisfactory explanation of this lack of hospitality in the French. I put it down first to the cost of living, then to the limited accommodation, then to the disobliging servants, but I have now come to the conclusion that it is one of their national characteristics, and it is useless to waste time trying to explain it.

Let us know as soon as possible when you are coming.

.      .      .      .      .      .

After the description I have given you of our life in Smyrna you will understand how sorry we were to return to Constantinople. Even the delight of again seeing our parents could not console us. As soon as we were back again began the same monotony and perpetual dread,

MELEK IN YASHMAK

and the Hamidian régime made life more and more impossible.

The year that the Belgian anarchist tried to kill the Sultan Hamid, was certainly the worst I have ever spent. Even the Armenian Massacres, which were amongst the most haunting and horrible souvenirs of our youth, could not be compared with what we had then to bear. Arrests went on wholesale! Thousands were " suspect," questioned, tortured perhaps. And when the real culprit had declared his guilt before the whole tribunal and had proved that it was he, and he alone, who had thrown the bomb, the poor prisoners were not released.

It was in the summer. Up till then in the country, a woman could go out in the evening, if she were accompanied, but this was at once prohibited ; every Turkish boat which was not a fishing boat was stopped ; in the streets all those who could not prove the reason for being out were arrested ; no longer were visits to the Embassies possible, no longer could the ladies from the Embassies come to see us ; no " white dinners," no meeting of friends. There were police stationed before the doors, and we dared not play the piano for fear of appearing too

gay, when our "Sovereign Lord's " life had been
in danger.

Of course no letters could be received from
our Western friends. The foreign posts were
searched through and through, and nearly all
the movement of the daily life was at an end.
One evening my sister and I went outside to
look at the moonlit Bosphorus. Although accompanied by a male relative, three faithful guardians
of the safety of our beloved Monarch stepped
forward and asked for explanations as to why
we were gazing at the sea. Not wishing to
reply, we were asked to follow them to the
nearest police station. My sister and I went in,
leaving our relative to explain matters, and I
can assure you that was the last time we dared
to study moon effects. Never, I think, more
than that evening, was I so decided to leave
our country, come what might ! Life was just
one perpetual nightmare, and for a long time
after, even now in security, I still dream of
these days of terror.

I remember full well what importance was
given to the French 1st of May riots. When I
myself saw one of the strikers throw a stone
which nearly blinded a doctor, called in haste

to see a patient, and saw his motor stopped
and broken to pieces and the chauffeur thrashed,
I thought of the days of our Armenian massacres
—the awful days of Hamidian carnage—and the
1st of May riots seemed to me a Revolution
arranged to amuse little children.—Your affectionate                                     ZEYNEB.

# CHAPTER XIV
## A STUDY IN CONTRASTS

K

# CHAPTER XIV

## A STUDY IN CONTRASTS

NICE, *March* 1907.

THERE are habits, my dearest friend, which cannot be lost in the West any more than they can be acquired in the East. You know what a terrible task it is for a Turkish woman to write a letter—even a Turkish woman who pretends to be Western in many ways. Can you, who belong to a race which can quietly take a decision and act upon it, understand this fault of ours, which consists of always putting off till the morrow what should be done the same day? Thanks to this laziness, we Turks are where we are to-day. Some people call it *kismet;* you can find it in almost all our actions. Since we started, now a year ago, I have been expecting an answer to a letter sent the day after my arrival here. It will come; Allah knows when, but it will come.

But I am as bad as my friend, you will say.

Three weeks ago I began this letter to you, and it is not finished yet, for all I am doing is so strange and curious, I feel I must let you know all about it.

It was at Monte Carlo that I first saw and heard the wonderful operas of Wagner. When I heard they were performing *Rheingold*, in spite of medical advice not to go into a theatre, I could not keep away. Since my childhood, I had longed to hear an orchestral interpretation of the works of this genius. I seemed to have a presentiment that it would be to me an incomparable revelation, and I was not disappointed.

Do you know what it is, to have loved music all your life and never to have an opportunity of hearing a first-class concert ? My father used to invite the distinguished women artistes, passing through Constantinople, to come to sing and play for us. He, too, was passionately fond of music. But what I longed above all to hear was a full orchestra, and Wagner ! So that, when I was actually at Monte Carlo listening to the entrancing work of this Master, it was as though I had been blind all my days and had at last received my sight.

It was wonderful ! It was magnificent ! It

moved my very soul ! Why should we regret having left our country when such masterpieces as this are yet to be heard ?

I did not want to stir. I wanted to remain under the spell of that glorious music ! But the theatre authorities thought differently, and in a little while the beautiful performance of *Rheingold* became one of my most happy memories.

.     .     .     .     .     .

The scene changes. From my first beautiful impression of music I came to look upon that most degrading spectacle of your Western civilisation—I mean gambling. I had never realised till now that collective robbery could be so shameful ! That a poor, unintelligent, characterless being can come to Monte Carlo, ruin himself and his family, and kill himself without anyone taking the trouble to pity him a little or have him treated like a sick man, is to me incomprehensible. When I told the lady and gentleman, who accompanied me, the impression that their gaming-tables had on me, they smiled ; indeed they made an effort not to laugh.

I remained long enough to study that strange

collection of heads round the table with their expressions all so different, but the most hideous which I have ever seen.

I had received that day two new and very different impressions ; one the impression of the highest form of art and the other the impression of perhaps the saddest of all modern vices.

The whole night through I was torn between these two impressions. Which would get the better of me ? I tried to hum little passages of *Rheingold,* and fix my attention on Wagner's opera and the joy it had been to me, but in spite of my efforts my thoughts wandered, and I was far away in Turkey.

In our cloistered homes I had heard vague rumours of magic games, the players at which lost their all or made a colossal fortune according to the caprice of fate. But I did not pay much attention to this fairy tale. Now, however, I have seen and believe, and a feeling of terrible anxiety comes over me whenever I think of the honest men of my own country, who are concentrating all their energies on the acquirement of Western civilisation. They will not accept Europeanism in moderate doses—

they will drain the cup to the very dregs—this awful vice, as well as drunkenness and all your other weaknesses.

In the course of time I fell asleep. I was back in Turkey enduring the horrors of the Hamidian régime. *Rheingold* was forgotten, and the azure of the Mediterranean Sea, the flowers, and the summer dresses. I went from scene to scene, one more awful than the other, but everywhere I went and to everything I saw were attached the diabolical faces I had seen at the Monte Carlo gaming-tables.—Your affectionate                              ZEYNEB.

# CHAPTER XV
## DREAMS AND REALITIES

# CHAPTER XV

## DREAMS AND REALITIES

HENDAYE, July 1907.

WHAT a relief! What a heart-felt relief to leave Paris! Paris with its noise and clamour and perpetual and useless movement! Paris which is so different from what I expected!

We have had in Paris what you English people call a " season," and I shall require many months of complete rest, to get over the effects of that awful modern whirlwind.

What an exhausting life! What unnecessary labour! And what a contrast to our calm harem existence away yonder. I think—yes, I almost think I have had enough of the West now, and want to return to the East, just to get back the old experience of calm.

Picture to yourself the number of new faces we have seen in six weeks. What a collection of women—chattering, irritating, inquisitive, demonstrative, and obliging women, who invite you again and again, and when you do go to their receptions you get nothing for your trouble but crowding and pushing.

All the men and women in Paris are of uncertain years. The pale girl who serves the tea might be of any age from fifteen to thirty, and the men with the well-trimmed fingers and timid manners are certainly not sixty, but they might be anything up to forty.

But where are the few *intellectuelles*? Lost between the lace and the teacups. They look almost ashamed of being seen there at all. They have real knowledge, and to meet them is like opening the chapter of a valuable Encyclopedia; but hardly has one taken in the discovery, when one is pushed along to find the conclusion of the chapter somewhere in the crowd, if indeed it can be found.

As you know, since our arrival from Nice we have not had one free evening. The *Grandes Dames* of France wanted to get a closer view of two Turkish women, and they have all been charming to us, especially the elder ones.

Yes, charming is the word which best applies to all these society ladies, young and old, and is not *to be charming* the modern ideal of civilisation ? These women are all physically the model of a big Paris dressmaker, and morally what society allows them to be—some one quite inoffensive. But it is not their fault that they have all been formed on the same pattern, and that those who have originality hide it under the same exterior as the others, fearful lest such a blemish should even be suspected !

But really, am I not a little pedantic ? How can I dare to come to such a conclusion after a visit which lasts barely a quarter of an hour ?

At luncheon and dinner the favourite topics of conversation are the pieces played at the theatres or the newest books. Marriage, too, is always an interesting subject, and everyone seems eager to get married in spite of the thousand and one living examples there are to warn others of what it really is. This supreme trust in a benign Fate amuses me. Every bride-elect imagines it is she who will be the one exception to the general rule. Turkish women do not look forward to matrimony with the same confidence.

Divorce has a morbid fascination for the men and women here : so have other people's misfortunes. And as soon as a man or woman is down—a woman particularly—everyone delights in giving his or her contribution to the moral kicking.

I must own, too, I cannot become enthusiastic about Mdlle. Cecile Sorel's clothes nor the grace of a certain Russian dancer. What I would like to talk about would be some subject which could help us two peoples to understand each other better, but such subjects are carefully avoided as tiresome.

Do you remember how anxious we were to hear Strauss's *Salome* discussed, and what it was in all this work which interested these Paris Society ladies ?—nothing more nor less than whether it was Trohohanova or Zambelli who was to dance the part of Salome.

That was a disappointment for me ! All my life I looked forward to being in a town where music was given the place of honour, for in Constantinople, as you know, there is music for everyone except the Turkish woman.

I had no particular desire to see the monuments of Paris, and now I have visited them my affection for them is only lukewarm. The Philistine I am ! I wish I dared tell the Parisians what I really thought of them and

their beautiful Paris! I had come above all
things to educate myself in music, and now I
find that they, with their unbounded oppor-
tunities, have shamefully failed to avail themselves of what to me, as a Turkish woman, is
the great chance of a lifetime.

A WALK WITH PIERRE LOTI IN A
WESTERN CEMETERY

Yesterday afternoon, accompanied by M.
Pierre Loti, we visited the cemetery of Bir-
reyatou. Its likeness to Turkey attracted us
at once, for all that is Eastern has a peculiar
fascination for Loti. There were the same
cypress trees and plants that grow in our cemeteries, and the tombs were cared for in a manner
which is quite unusual in Western Europe.

To go for a walk in a burial-ground I know
is exclusively an Eastern form of amusement.
But wait till you have seen our cemeteries and
compared them with your own, then you will
understand better this taste of ours. Oh, the
impression of loneliness and horror I felt when
I first saw a Western cemetery! It was Père
La Chaise, the most important of them all. I

went there to steal a leaf from the famous weeping willow on Musset's grave, and to my great surprise I found by the Master's tomb, amongst other tokens of respect, a Russian girl's visiting card with the corner turned down. But this was an exception. How you Western people neglect your dead !

I could not for a long time explain to myself this fear of death, but since I have seen here the painful scenes connected with it—the terror of Extreme Unction,[1] the visit of the relatives to the dead body, the funeral pomp, the hideous black decorations on the horses' heads, and last but not least the heart-rending mourning—I, too, am terrified.

We, like the Buddhists, have no mourning. The Angel of Death takes our dear ones from us to a happier place, and night and morning we pray for them. The coffin is carried out on men's shoulders in the simplest manner possible, and the relatives in the afternoon take their embroidery and keep the dear ones company. It is as if they were being watched in their sleep, and they are very, very near.

[1] The editor is not responsible for the ideas expressed in this book, which are not necessarily her own.

ZEYNEB IN HER WESTERN DRAWING ROOM

She is playing the oute, or Turkish guitar, which is played with a feather. Although Turkish women are now good pianists and fond of Western music, they generally like to play the oute at least once a day.

Yet here in the West what a difference ! I shudder at the thought that some day I might have to rest in one of these untidy waste heaps, and that idea has been preying on my mind so that I have actually written to my father and begged him, should I die in Paris, to have me taken home and buried in a Turkish cemetery.

.        .        .        .        .        .

### COMÉDIE FRANÇAISE

Did I ever tell you of my visit to the Comédie Française ?    Alas, alas !  again I have to chronicle a disappointment.  I am trying to think what I pictured to myself I was going to see, and I am not at all clear about it.    In my childish imagination I must have thought of something I will *never* see.

Naturally the piece played was *Œdipus Rex*. Every time I am invited to the Comédie Fran-çaise I see *Œdipus Rex*.  It seems a particular favourite in Paris, I am  sure  I cannot  tell why.

The scenery was perfect, so were the costumes, but you cannot imagine how uncomfortable I was when I heard the actors, together or one after the other, screaming, moaning, hissing, and

L

calling on the whole audience to witness a misfortune, which was only too obvious.

All the actors were breathless, hoarse, exhausted—in sympathy I was exhausted too, and longed for the *entr'acte*. Then when at last a pause did come, I began to hope in the next scene a little calm would be established and the actors take their task a little more leisurely. But no ! they cried out louder still, threw themselves about in torture, and gesticulated with twice as much violence.

When I heard the voice of Œdipus it reminded me of the night watchers in my own country giving the fire alarm, and all those Turks who have heard it are of the same opinion. As I left the theatre tired out, I said to myself, "Surely it is not possible that this is the idea the Greeks had of Dramatic Art."

What a difference to the theatre I had known in Turkey ! Sometimes our mothers organised excursions, and we were taken in long springless carts, dragged by oxen, to the field of Conche-Dili in the valley of Chalcedonia, where there was a kind of theatre, or caricature of a theatre, built of unpainted wood, which held about four hundred people.

The troop was composed of Armenian men and women who had never been at the Paris Conservatoire, but who gave a fine interpretation of the works of Dumas, Ohnet, Octave Feuillet, and Courteline. The stage was small and the scenery was far from perfect, but the Moslem women were delighted with this open-air theatre, although they had to sit in latticed boxes and the men occupied the best seats in the stalls.

During the *entr'acte*, there was music and singing, the orchestra being composed of six persons who played upon stringed instruments. The conductor beat time on a big drum, and sometimes he sang songs of such intense sadness that we wondered almost whence they came.

That was a dear little theatre, the theatre of my childhood. Primitive though it was, it was very near to me as I listened to the piercing cries of alarm sent out by Œdipus. Would they not, these rustic actors of the Chalcedonian valley, I wonder, have given a truer and better interpretation of the plays of Sophocles?

.    .    .    .    .    .

A BULL-FIGHT

Guess, my dear, where I have been this afternoon. Guess, guess! I, a Turkish woman, have been to a bull-fight! There were many English people present. They are, I am told, the *habitués* of the place, and they come away, like the Spaniards, almost intoxicated by the spectacle.

This is an excitement which does not in the least appeal to me. Surely one must be either prehistoric or decadent to get into this unwholesome condition of the Spaniards. Is the sight of a bull which is being killed, and perhaps the death of a toreador, " *such a delightful show,*" to quote the exact words of my American neighbour ? He shouted with frenzy whilst my sister and two Poles, unable to bear the sight of the horses' obtruding intestines, had to be led out of the place in an almost fainting condition.

As for myself, I admit to having admired two things, the suppleness of the men and the brilliant appearance of the bull-ring. The women of course lent a picturesque note to the *ensemble* with their sparkling jewels, their faces radiant as those of the men, their dark

eyes dancing with excitement, and their handsome gowns and their graceful mantillas. But
shall I ever forget the hideous sight of the poor
horse staggering out of the ring, nor the roars
of the wounded bull ? It was a spectacle awful to
look upon. What a strange performance for a
Turkish woman, used to the quiet of our harem
life !

Perhaps, however, for those to whom life has
brought no emotion or sorrow, no joy or love,
those who have never seen the wholesale butchery
to which we, alas ! had almost become accustomed—perhaps to these people this horrible
sight is a necessity. Spanish writers have told
me they have done their best work after a bull-
fight, and before taking any important step in
life they needed this stimulus to carry them
safely through. I can assure you, however, I
heaved a sigh of relief when the performance
was over, and not for untold gold would I ever
go to see it again.

After leaving the scene I have described to
you, we followed the crowd to a little garden
planted with trees, which is situated in the
Calle Mayor and stretches along the side of the
stream till it meets the Bidassoa. This is the

spot where, on cool evenings, men and maidens meet to dance the Fandango. Basque men with red caps are seated in the middle to supply the music. On the sandy earth, which is the ball-room, the couples dance, in and out of the gnarled trees, to the rhythm of dance music, that is strange and passionate and at the same time almost languishing.

The music played was more Arabian than anything I have yet heard in the West, but unfortunately the modern note too was creeping into these delightful measures. The Basques with their red caps, bronzed faces, white teeth, and fine manly figures, the women with their passionate and supple movements and deco-rated mantillas, and the almost antique frame of Fontarabia, proud of its past, hopeful for its future, were all so new and so different to me.

But it is dark now, the dancing has ceased, the crowd has dispersed. How good it is to be out at this hour of the evening. I, who am free (or think I am), delight in the fact there are no Turkish policemen to question me as to what I am doing.

.    .    .    .    .    .

But alas! alas! I spoke of my freedom a

little too soon.  Even in this quiet city can I not pass unobserved ?

" Have you anything to declare ? " a Custom House officer asks me.

" Yes," I replied, " my hatred of your Western ' Customs,' and my delight at being alive."— Your affectionate friend,  ZEYNEB.

# CHAPTER XVI

## THE MOON OF RAMAZAN

# CHAPTER XVI

## THE MOON OF RAMAZAN

HENDAYE, *August* 1907.

YOU ask me to describe the life a Turkish woman leads during Ramazan.

The evenings of Ramazan are the only evenings of the year when she has the right to be out of doors ; the time when she seizes every opportunity of meeting her friends and arranging interesting soirées ; the time when she goes on foot or drives to the Mosques to hear the Imams explain the Word of the Prophet.

Need I remind you, unlike the women of the lower and middle classes, who go out *every* evening, the more important the family to which a woman belongs, the more difficult is it for her to go out.

It is for the evenings of Ramazan that most amusements are arranged, and our husbands, fathers, and brothers usually patronise the travelling circus, Turkish theatre, performances of Karakheuz.[1]  The women on their side have their dinners, Oriental dancing, and conversation which lasts deep into the night.

Amongst my most delightful remembrances of Constantinople are the Ramazan visits to St. Sophia and the Chah-zade Mosque. From the height of a gallery reserved for women, which is separated from the rest of the church by a thick wooden lattice-work, hundreds of " Believers " are to be seen, seated on the ground round the Imam, who reads and preaches to them.  All the oil lamps are lighted for the thirty days, and the incense burning in the silver brasiers rises with the prayers to Heaven. Not a voice is to be heard save that of the Imam (preacher), and the most wonderful impression of all is that created by the profound silence.

And yet children are there—little ones asleep in their mother's arms, little girls in the women's gallery, whilst boys over eight are counted men, and sit beside their fathers on the ground, their little legs tucked under them.

On returning home supper is ready for three o'clock, and an hour later the cannon announce

[1] Karakheuz = Turkish performance similar to our Punch and Judy Show.

TURKISH LADIES PAYING A VISIT

Every visitor is given coffee and cigarettes on arriving. The three ladies shown are Zeyneb, Melek, and a friend seated between them. A verse from the Koran hangs on the wall.

the commencement of a fresh day of fasting. After a short prayer in one's own room, sleep takes possession of us until late the next day, sometimes until almost four o'clock, when everyone must be up and again ready for the firing of the cannon which gives permission to eat and drink and smoke.

With us fasting [1] is more strict than it is in the West. From sunrise to sunset, no one would dare to touch a mouthful of food or even smoke.

When we are lucky enough to have Ramazan during the winter months the fasting hours are shorter, but when it comes in the month of August " Believers " have to fast for sixteen hours, and the labourers suffer much in consequence.

Imagine how long a soirée can be, when you begin dinner at half-past four ! What must we not think of to amuse our guests, for no one dines alone ! The Oriental hospitality demands that every evening friends should assemble, and acquaintances come without even letting you know. When people are known to be rich,

[1] Zeyneb has forgotten that as well as Fridays and various fast days, every Catholic receives the Holy Communion fasting.—G. E.

the poor and complete strangers come to them to dinner. I remember being at one house which was filled to overflowing with women of all classes, most of whom had never before even seen the hostess.

At the Palaces a special door is built, through which anyone who wants to dine can enter, and after the meal money is distributed. You can understand while this patriarchal system exists there is no reason for the poor to envy the rich. Turkey is the only country in Europe which in this respect lives according to Christ's teaching, but no doubt in the march of progress all these beautiful customs will disappear.

I have often thought when in a Western drawing-room, where one stays a few minutes, and eats perhaps a sandwich, how different are our receptions in the East. We meet without being invited, talk till late in the night, and a proper supper is served.

It surprises me, too, in the West to meet such poor linguists. In Turkey it is quite usual to hear discussions going on in five European languages without one foreigner being present.

Wait till you have taken part in some of these Ramazan gatherings, and have seen what hospitality really is, then you will understand my rather slighting remarks about your Western society.

．　　　．　　　．　　　．　　　．　　　．

I am constantly being asked how a Turkish woman amuses herself. I have a stock answer ready: "That depends on what you call amusement."

It sounds futile to have to remind my questioners that amusement is a relative quality, and depends entirely on one's personal tastes. The Spaniards are mad with delight at the sight of a bull-fight—to me it was disgusting; and yet, probably, were those bull-fights to take place in Turkey, I should enjoy them. We used to have in the country exhibitions of wrestling at which whole families were present. Travelling circuses were also a favourite amusement, but during the last years of Hamid's reign Turkish women have been forbidden the pleasures of going to a travelling theatre and Karakheuz, the most appreciated of all the Eastern amusements.

Tennis, croquet, and other games are impossible for us, neither is rowing allowed: to have indulged in that sport was to expose myself to the criticism of the whole capital.

Although the people of the West are so fond of walking as a recreation, the pleasure that a *Turkish* woman can obtain from a walk is practically non-existent, and most of us would be insulted if asked, as I have been in Paris, to walk for two hours.

We are fond of swimming, but how is this taste to be indulged when women are only allowed to swim in an enclosed place, surrounded by a high wall? Surely the only charm of swimming is to be in the open sea.

Those who are fond of music have either to go without, learn to play themselves, or take the terrible risk of disguising themselves as Europeans and go to a concert.

Towards 1876 we began playing bezique, but that craze did not last long, and a short time afterwards cards were considered bad form. The *Perotes*,[1] however, still remain faithful to card-playing, and have more than one reason to prefer this pastime to all the others in which they might indulge. Unlike the *Perotes*, we Turkish women never played cards for money.

---

[1] Inhabitants of Pera. There is no love lost between these ladies and the Turkish women proper. I personally found many of them very charming.—G. E.

You might think from my letters that travelling in the country was quite an ordinary event for women of our class : on the contrary, it is quite exceptional, and perhaps only ten families in all Turkey have travelled as we travelled in our own country.

So you see a Turkish woman is not very ambitious for " amusement " as you Western people understand the word. When she is allowed to travel in foreign countries as she likes, I believe she will be more satisfied with her lot.

All the Turks I have met since I came to Europe are of my opinion, but we shall see what will happen when their theories are put into practice.

Since it has been my privilege to meet my countrymen I have found out what fine qualities they possess. Indeed it is wrong for custom to divide so markedly our nation into two sexes and to create such insuperable barriers between them. We shall never be strong until we are looked upon as one, and can mix freely together. The Turks have all the qualities necessary to make good husbands and fathers, and yet we have no opportunity of knowing even the men we marry until we *are* married.

M

How I wish that nine out of every ten of the books written on Turkey could be burned! How unjustly the Turk has been criticised! And what nonsense has been written about the women! I cannot imagine where the writers get their information from, or what class of women they visited. Every book I have read has been in some way unfair to the Turkish woman. Not one woman has really understood us! Not one woman has credited us with the possession of a heart, a mind, or a soul.—Your affectionate friend, ZEYNEB.

---

The year of 1908 was a year of mourning for Zeyneb and Melek. For them began that bitter period, when a woman has the opportunity of judging independence at its true value, without a father and a substantial income as buffers between them and life.

.    .    .    .    .    .

During that year, too, Melek married. Zeyneb remained alone.

# CHAPTER XVII
## AND IS THIS REALLY FREEDOM?

# CHAPTER XVII

## AND IS THIS REALLY FREEDOM ?

LONDON, *Nov.-Dec.* 1908.

ABOUT a week ago,[1] whilst you were writing your first letter to me and speaking of the beautiful Eastern sun that was shining through your latticed window, what a different experience was mine in London. I was walking by myself in the West End, when suddenly, the whole city was shrouded in one of those dense fogs to which you no doubt have become accustomed. I could not see the name of the streets nor the path at the opposite side, so I wandered on for a little while, only to discover that I had arrived back at the same place.

There was no one to show me the way, and the English language that I had spoken from

---

[1] I received this letter in Constantinople, where I was staying in a Turkish harem, having travelled there in order to be present at the first debate in the newly-opened Turkish Parliament.—G. E.

181

infancy seemed of no use to me, since no one took any notice of my questions.

I looked in vain for a policeman. Your London policemen are so amiable and clever. Whatever difficulty I have, they seem to be able to help me, and the most curious of all curious things is, they will not accept tips! What wonderful men! and what a difference from our policemen in Constantinople! In Constantinople, I trembled almost at the sight of a policeman, but here I cannot imagine what I should do without them.

However, after losing myself and getting back always to the same point, I finally struck out in a new direction, and walked on and on until, when I was least expecting it, I found that just by chance I was safe in front of my club. You can perhaps imagine my relief. It seemed to me as if I had escaped from some terrible danger, and I wonder more and more how you English people manage to find your way in one of these dense fogs.

When I got into my club, I found your letter waiting me, and the Turkish post-mark cheered me just a little, and made me forget for a while the hideous black mantle in which London was wrapt.

On those evenings when I dine at " my club " (see how English I have become!) I eat alone, studying all the time the people I see around me. What a curious harem! and what a difference from the one in which you are living at present.

The first time I dined there I ordered the vegetarian dinner, expecting to have one of those delicious meals which you are enjoying (you lucky woman!), which consists of everything that is good. But alas! the food in this harem has been a disappointment to me. Surely I must not accept this menu as a sample of what English food really is.

On a little table all to myself, I was served with, first of all, rice which was cooked not as in Turkey, and as a second course I had carrots cooked in water! After sprinkling on them quantities of salt and pepper I could not even then swallow them, so I asked for pickles, but as there were none, that dish was sent away almost untouched to join the first. Next I was served with a compote of pears without sugar, but that also did not come up to my expectations. I ate up, however, all my bread and asked for more. Then the waiter kindly went from table to table to see how much he could collect, brought just a handful, and informed me he really could not give me any more. But I told him it was not enough. " I want a very large piece," I said, so finally he decided to consult the butler, went to the kitchen, and brought me back a loaf to myself.

All this while, the curious people around me had been staring at me devouring my loaf, but after a while they wearied of that exciting entertainment, their faces again resumed their usual calm expression, and they went on once more talking to one another. Sometimes, but not often, they almost got interested in their neighbour's remark, but as soon as the last words were uttered again they adopted a manner which seemed to me one of absolute indifference.

As you know, I do not swear by everything Turkish, but you must now admit from experience that when once the Danube is crossed the faces to be seen do express some emotion, either love or hate, contentment or disappointment, but not indifference. Since I left Belgrade, I have tried, almost in vain, to find in the Western faces the reflection of some personality, and so few examples have I found that their names would

ZEYNEB WITH A BLACK FACE-VEIL THROWN BACK

not certainly fill this page. Here in London I met with the same disappointment. Have these people really lost all interest in life? They give me the impression that they all belong to the same family, so much alike are they in appearance and in facial expression.

In the reading-room, where I spent my evening, I met those same people, who spoke in whispers, wrote letters, and read the daily papers. The silence of the room was restful, there was an atmosphere almost of peace, but it is not the peace which follows strife, it is the peace of apathy. Is this, then, what the Turkish women dream of becoming one day? Is this their ideal of independence and liberty?

Were you to show my letter to one of my race she would think that I had a distinct aversion for progress, or that I felt obliged to be in opposition to everything in the countries where I was travelling. You know enough of my life, however, to know that this is not the case. What I do feel, though, is that a *Ladies' Club* is not a big enough reward for having broken away from an Eastern harem and all the suffering that has been the consequence of that action. A club, as I said before, is after all another kind of harem, but it has none of the mystery and charm of the Harem of the East.

How is one to learn and teach others what might perhaps be called " the tact of evolution " —I mean the art of knowing when to stop even in the realm of progress ?

I cannot yet either analyse or classify in a satisfactory way your methods of thinking, since in changing from country to country even the words alter their meaning. In Servia, Liberal means Conservative, and Freemason on the Continent has quite a different meaning from what it has here ; so that the interpretation I would give to an opinion might fail to cover my real meaning.

Do not think that this evening's pessimism is due to the fog nor to my poor dinner. It is the outcome of disillusions which every day become more complete. It seems to me that we Orientals are children to whom fairy tales have been told for too long—fairy tales which have every appearance of truth. You hear so much of the *mirage* of the East, but what is that compared to the *mirage* of the West, to which all Orientals are attracted ?

They tell you fairy tales, too, you women of the West—fairy tales which, like ours, have all the appearance of truth. I wonder, when the Englishwomen have really won their vote and the right to exercise all the tiring professions of men, what they will have gained? Their faces will be a little sadder, a little more weary, and they will have become wholly disillusioned.

Go to the root of things and you will find the more things change the more they are the same; nothing really changes. Human nature is always the same. We cannot stop the ebb or flow of Time, however much we try. The great mass of mediocrity alone is happy, for it is content to swim with the tide. Does it not seem to you, that each of us from the age when we begin to reason feels more or less the futility and uselessness of some of our efforts; the little good that struggling has brought us, and the danger we necessarily run, in this awful desire to go full speed ahead? And yet, this desire to go towards something, futile though it be, is one of the most indestructible of Western sentiments.

When in Turkey we met together, and spoke of the Women of England, we imagined that they had nothing more to wish for in this world. But we had no idea of what the struggle for life meant to them, nor how terrible was this eternal search after happiness. Which is the harder struggle of the two ?  The latter is the only struggle we know in Turkey, and the same futile struggle goes on all the world over.

Happiness—what a mirage !  At best is it not a mere negation of pain, for each one's idea of happiness is so different ?  When I was fifteen years old they made me a present of a little native from Central Africa.  For her there was no greater torture than to wear garments of any kind, and her idea of happiness was to get back to the home on the borders of Lake Chad and the possibility of eating another roasted European.

.        .        .        .        .        .

Last night I went to a banquet.  It was the first time that I had ever heard after-dinner speeches, and I admired the ease with which everyone found something to say, and the women spoke quite as well as the men.  Afterwards I was told, however, that these speeches had all been prepared beforehand.

The member of Parliament who sat on my

right spoilt my evening's enjoyment by making
me believe I had to speak, and all through the
dinner I tried to find something to say, and yet
I knew that, were I actually to rise, I could not
utter a sound. What most astonished me at
that banquet, however, was that all those women,
who made no secret of wanting to direct the
affairs of the nation, dared not take the responsibility of smoking until they were told. What a
contradiction !

Since I came here I have seen nothing but
" Votes for Women " chalked all over the pave-
ments and walls of the town. These methods
of propaganda are all so new to me.

I went to a Suffrage street corner meeting the
other night, and I can assure you I never want
to go again. The speaker carried her little stool
herself, another carried a flag, and yet a third
woman a bundle of leaflets and papers to dis-
tribute to the crowd. After walking for a little
while they placed the stool outside a dirty-looking
public-house, and the lady who carried the flag
boldly got on to the stool and began to shout,
not waiting till the people came to hear her,
so anxious was she to begin. Although she did
not look nervous in the least she possibly was,

for her speech came abruptly to an end, and my heart began to beat in sympathy with her.

When the other lady began to speak quite a big crowd of men and women assembled: degraded-looking ruffians they were, most of them, and a class of man I had not yet seen. All the time they interrupted her, but she went bravely on, returning their rudeness with sarcasm. What an insult to womanhood it seemed to me, to have to bandy words with this vulgar mob. One man told her that " she was ugly." Another asked " if she had done her washing," but the most of their hateful remarks I could not understand, so different was their English from the English I had learned in Turkey.

Yet how I admired the courage of that woman ! No physical pain could be more awful to me than not to be taken for a lady, and this speaker of such remarkable eloquence and culture was not taken for a lady by the crowd, seeing she was supposed " to do her own washing " like any women of the people.

The most pitiful part of it all to me is the blind faith these women have in their cause, and the confidence they have that in explaining their policy to the street ruffians, who cannot even understand that they are ladies, they will further their cause by half an inch.

I was glad when the meeting was over, but sorry that such rhetoric should have been wasted on the half-intoxicated loungers who deigned to come out of the public-house and listen. If this is what the women of your country have to bear in their fight for freedom, all honour to them, but I would rather groan in bondage.

. . . . . .

I have been to see your famous Houses of Parliament, both the Lords and the Commons. Like all the architecture in London, these buildings create such an atmosphere of kingly greatness in which I, the democrat of my own country, am revelling. The Democracy of the East is so different from that of the West, of which I had so pitiful an example at the street corner.

I was invited to tea at the House of Commons, and to be invited to tea there of all places seemed very strange to me. Is the drinking of tea of such vital importance that the English can *never* do without it ? I wonder if the Turks, now *their* Parliament is opened, will drink coffee with ladies instead of attending to the laws of the nation !

What a long, weary wait I had before they would let me into the Houses of Parliament. Every time I asked the policeman where the member of Parliament was who had invited me, he smilingly told me they had gone to fetch him. I thought he was joking at first, and threatened to go, but he only laughed, and said, "He will come in time." Only when I had made up my mind that the tea-party would never come off, and had settled myself on an uncomfortable divan to study the curious people passing in and out, did my host appear. I thought it was only in Turkey that appointments were kept with such laxity, but I was reminded by the M.P. who invited me that I was three-quarters of an hour late in the first place.

I was conducted through a long, handsome corridor to a lobby where all sorts of men and women were assembled, pushing one another, gesticulating and speaking in loud, disagreeable voices like those outside of the Paris Bourse. Just then, however, a bell rang, and I was conducted back past the policeman to my original seat. What curious behaviour! What did it all mean? I spoke to the friendly policeman, but

A CORNER OF A TURKISH HAREM OF TO-DAY

This photograph was taken expressly for a London paper. It was returned with this comment : "The British public would not accept this as a picture of a Turkish Harem." As a matter of fact, in the smartest Turkish houses European furniture is much in evidence.

TURKISH WOMEN AND CHILDREN IN THE COUNTRY

They are accompanied by the negress.

his explanation that they were " dividing " did not convey much to my mind.   As I stood there, a stray member of Parliament came and looked at me.   He must have been a great admirer of Mr. Joseph Chamberlain, for he wore a monocle and an orchid in his buttonhole.

" Are these suffragettes ? " he asked the policeman, staring at me and the other women.

" No, sir," answered the policeman, " ladies."

It was too late for tea when my host returned to fetch me, but the loss of a cup of tea is no calamity to me, as I only drink it to appear polite.   I was next taken up to the Ladies' Gallery, and was sworn in as one of the relations of a member who had given up his ladies' tickets to my host.   The funny part of it was, that I could not understand the language my relation spoke, so different was his English from the English I had learnt in Turkey.   But what a fuss to get into that Ladies' Gallery !   I had no idea of making a noise before it was suggested to my mind by making me sign a book, and I certainly wanted to afterwards.   What unnecessary trouble !   What do you call it ?   Red tapeism ! One might almost be in Turkey under Hamid and not in Free England.

N

But, my dear, why have you never told me that the Ladies' Gallery is a harem? A harem with its latticed windows! The harem of the Government! No wonder the women cried through the windows of that harem that they wanted to be free! I felt inclined to shout out too. "Is it in Free England that you dare to have a harem? How inconsistent are you English! You send your women out unprotected all over the world, and here in the workshop where your laws are made, you cover them with a symbol of protection."

The performance which I saw through the harem windows was boring enough. The humbler members of the House had little respect for their superiors, seeing they sat in their presence with their hats on, and this I am told was the habit of a very ill-bred man. Still perhaps this attitude does not astonish me since on all sides I hear complaints of the Government. It is a bad sign for a country, my dear. Are you following in Turkey's footsteps? Hatred of the Government and prison an honour! Poor England!

I was very anxious to see the notorious Mr. Lloyd George. Since I have been in London his name is on everyone's lips. I have heard very little good of him except from the ruffians at the street corner meeting, and yet like our Hamid he seems to be all-powerful. For a long time, I could not distinguish him in the crowd below, although my companion spared no pains in pointing him out. I was looking for some one with a commanding presence, some one with an eagle eye and a wicked face like our Sultan, some one before whom a whole nation was justified in trembling. But I still wonder whether I am thinking of the right man when I think of Mr. Lloyd George.

There is not much excitement in your House of Commons, is there? I prefer the Chamber of Deputies, even though some one fired at M. Briand the day I went there. There at least they are men of action. Here some members were so weary of law-making, that they crossed their legs, folded their arms, and went to sleep whilst their colleagues opposite were speaking. I thought it would have been more polite to have gone out and taken tea, as the other members seemed to be doing all the time. It would have given them strength to listen to the tiresome debate.

To me, perhaps, the speaking would have been less unbearable if the harem windows had not deadened the sound, which, please notice, is my polite Turkish way of saying, they all spoke so indistinctly.

The bell began to ring again. The members of Parliament all walked towards the harem to this curious direction, "Eyes to the right and nose to the left." [1]   And at last my friend took me away.

. . . . . .

We went to see a performance of *Trilby* at His Majesty's Theatre the other night. I liked the acting of the terrible Svengali, but not the piece. As a great treat to me, my friend and her husband had us invited to supper in the roof of the theatre with the famous Sir Herbert Tree. I could not help saying, " I preferred not to go, for Sir Herbert Tree frightened me."

However, we went all the same, and had a delightful supper-party. For some reason or other the manager was our host, and I was thankful not to eat with Sir Herbert Tree. As we came away my friend asked if I was still frightened now we had eaten with him.

" But we have not eaten with him," I said.

[1] I leave my friend's spelling unchanged —G. E.

" Indeed we have," she said.

" Is the person with whom we had supper the horrid Svengali ? " I asked.

" Why, of course," she answered, laughing.

As you know, this is not my first experience of a theatre, so there is no excuse for me. But I can assure you no one would ever dream that Svengali was made up. What a pity it would have been for me to have gone through life thinking of your famous actor as Svengali. I think that when actors have to play such disagreeable parts, they should show themselves to the public afterwards as they really are, or *not* put their names on the programme.

.    .    .    .    .    .

I saw another play at His Majesty's in which the principal rôles were played by children. You cannot imagine how delightful I found it, and what a change it was from the eternal *pièce à thèse* which I had become accustomed to see in Paris. The scenery indeed was a fairy panorama, and the piece charmingly interpreted. What astonished me was to see that both men and women took as much delight in it as the young folks. Only mothers in Paris would have brought their children to see such a moral play.

Ah, but I must tell you I have at last seen an Englishwoman who does not look weary of life. She is Miss Ellen Terry. How good it was to see her act. She was so natural and so full of fun, and enjoyed all she had to say and do, that her performance was a real joy to me. I wish I could have thanked her.

. . . . . .

I just love your hansom cabs. If I had money enough I would buy one for myself and drive about seeing London. You get the best view of everything in this way. When I first stepped into one I could not imagine where the coachman sat ; he called out to me from somewhere, but I could not find his voice, until he popped his fingers through a little trap door and knocked off my hat, for I cannot bear to pin on my hat.

" Here I am," he answered to my query, and he thought he had a mad-woman for a fare.

. . . . . .

One night when I returned to my club after the theatre, there was one lonely woman seated in the reading-room near the fire. She seemed to me to be the youngest of all the ladies, although you may say that was no guarantee against middle age. I don't know how it was we began to speak, since no one had introduced us, but she imagined I was a Frenchwoman, hence probably the explanation of the liberty she had taken in addressing me. Yet she looked so sad.

" You French," she said, " are used to sitting up a good deal later than we do here."

" I thought," I said, " the protocol did not bother about such trifles."

" Ah, now you are in the country of protocols and etiquette," she answered.

She must have been asking me questions only as an excuse to speak herself, because she took really no interest in my answers, and she kept on chattering and chattering because she did not want me to go away. She spoke of America and India and China and Japan, all of which countries she seemed to know as well as her own. Never have I met in my travels anyone so fond of talking, and yet at the same time with a *spleen* which made me almost tired.

I concluded that she was an independent woman, whose weariness must have been the result of constant struggling. She was all alone in the world; one of those poor creatures who might die in a top back-room without a soul belonging to her.   Her mind must have been saturated with theories, she must have known all the uncomfortable shocks which come from a changed position, and yet she was British enough to tremble before Public Opinion.

" But do you know why I travel so much ? " at last I had the opportunity of asking her. " Like Diogenes who tried to find a *Man*, I have been trying to find a FREE woman, but have not been successful."

I do not think she understood in the least what I meant.—Your affectionate friend,

ZEYNEB.

# CHAPTER XVIII

## THE CLASH OF CREEDS

# CHAPTER XVIII

## THE CLASH OF CREEDS

LONDON, *Jan.* 1909.

I AM indeed a *désenchantée.* I envy you even your reasonable illusions about us. We are hopelessly what we are. I have lost all mine about you, and you seem to me as hopelessly what you are.

The only difference between the spleen of London and the spleen of Constantinople is that the foundation of'the Turkish character is dry cynicism, whilst the Englishman's is inane doggedness without object. In his fatalism the Turk is a philosopher. Your Englishman calls himself a man of action, but he is a mere empiric.

I quite understand now, however, that you do not pity my countrywomen, not because they do not need pity, but because for years you have led only the life of the women of this country, women who start so courageously to fight life's battle and who ultimately have had to bury all their life's illusions. Now, I see only too well, there are beings for whom freedom becomes too heavy a burden to bear. The women I have met here, seem to have been striving all their lives to get away from everything—home, family, social conventions. They want the right to live alone, to travel as they like, to be responsible for their own lives. Yet when their ambition is realised, the only harvest they reap after a youth of struggle is that of disenchantment.

Yet I ask myself, is a lonely old age worth a youth of effort ? Have they not confused individual liberty, which is the right to live as one pleases, with true liberty, which to my Oriental mind is the right to choose one's own joys and forbearances ?

.        .        .        .        .        .

Is it not curious that here, in a Christian country, I see nothing of the religion of Christ ? And yet commentaries are not lacking. Every sect has the presumption to suppose its particular interpretation of the words of Christ is the only right interpretation, and Christians have changed the meaning of His words so much, and seen Christ through the prism of their own minds, that I, primitive being that I am, do not recognise in their tangled creeds the simple and beautiful teaching of Jesus of Nazareth, Son of the carpenter Joseph.

Sometimes it seems to me that the religion of Christ has been brought beyond the confines of absurdity. Would it not be better to try and follow the example of Christ than to waste time disputing whether He would approve of eating chocolate biscuits on fast-days and whether wild duck is a fasting diet, whilst duck of the farmyard is forbidden ? To me, all this seems profanely childish.

The impression these numerous creeds make on me is like that of members of the same family disputing with one another. What happens in the case of families happens in the case of religion. From these discussions over details follow, first mistrust, then dislike, then hatred, always to the detriment of the best interest of them all.

I went to a Nonconformist chapel the other evening, but I could not bring myself to realise that I was in a chapel at all. There was nothing divine or sacred either in the building or the service. It was more like a lecture by an eloquent professor. Nor did the congregation

worship as we worship in the East. It seemed
to me, as if it was not to worship God that they
were there, but to appease the anger of some
Northern Deity, cold, intolerant, and wrathful—
an idea of the Almighty which I shall never
understand.

It astonished me to hear the professor calling
those present " miserable sinners," and as I was
one of the congregation I was not a little hurt,
for I have nothing very serious on my conscience.
But the Catholics, in this respect, err as much
as the Protestants. Why this hysteria for sins
you have not committed ? Why this shame
of one's self, this exaggerated humility, this
continual fear ? Why should you stand
trembling before your Maker ?

While I was still inside the chapel, a lady
came up and was introduced to me. We walked
down the street together, and in the course of
conversation she discovered I was not even a
Nonconformist, nor a Roman Catholic, but a
heathen. And she at once began to pity me,
and show me the advantages of her religion.
But what could she teach me about Christ that
I did not already know ? Unfortunately for
her she knew nothing of the religion of Mahomet,

THE BALCONY AT THE BACK OF ZEYNEB'S HOUSE
The house is covered with wistaria.

ZEYNEB AND MELEK
The Yashmak is exceedingly becoming, the white tulle showing the lips to
great advantage

nor how broad-minded he was, nor with what admiration he had spoken of the crucified Jesus, and how we all loved Christ from Mahomet's interpretation of His life and work.[1]

. . . . . .

As usual here, as in other Christian countries, marriage seems an everlasting topic of interest. I was hardly seven years old when I was taken for the first time to a non-Turkish marriage. It was the wedding of some Greek farm-people our governess knew. We were present at the nuptial benediction, which took place inside the house and which seemed to me interminable. After that, everyone, including the bride, partook of copious refreshments. Then, when we had been taken for a drive in the country, we returned to dinner, which was served in front of the stable. After the meal we danced on the grass to the strains of a violin, accordion, and triangle. That is the only Christian marriage I had seen till 1908, and I was astonished to find how different a Christian wedding is here.

What is the use of an organ for marrying

[1] It may be reasonably urged in reply that Zeyneb's criticism of our Christianity is far from adequate. But I have preferred to present the impressions of a Turkish woman.—G. E.

people ? And twelve bridesmaids ? The bridal pair themselves look extremely uncomfortable at all this useless ceremonial, to which nobody pays any particular attention. Every bride and bridegroom must know how unnecessary are all these preparations, and how marriages bore friends. Yet they go on putting themselves to all this useless trouble, and for what ?

Each person invited, I am told, has to bring a present. What a wicked expense to put their friends to. Oh, vanity of vanities !

How is it possible not to admire the primitive Circassians, who when they love one another and wish to marry, walk off without consulting anyone but themselves ?

.        .        .        .        .        .

I am also disappointed at the manner in which divorce proceedings are conducted in England. What a quantity of unkind words and vile accusations ! What a low handling and throwing of mud at each other, what expense, what time and worry ! And all simply to prove that two people are not suited to live together.

To think that, with the possibility of such a life of tragedy, there are still people who have the courage to get married ! It seems to me there are some who take marriage too seriously, others who do not take it seriously enough, and that others again only take it seriously when one of the partners wants to be liberated.

How sad it is! And what good can be said of laws, the work of human beings, which not only do not help us in our misfortunes, but extend neither pity nor pardon to those who try to suffer a little less.

During the time I lived away yonder and suffered from a total absence of liberty, I imagined that Europe respected the happiness and the misfortunes of individuals. How horrible it is to find in the daily papers the names of people mercilessly branded by their fellow-men for having committed no other fault than that of trying to be less unhappy, for having the madness to wish to repair their wrecked existence. To publish the reports of the evidence, the sordid gossip of menials, the calumnies, the stolen letters, written under such different circumstances, in moments of happiness, in absolute confidence, or extreme mental agony, in which a woman has laid her soul bare, is loathsome. Is it not worse than perjury to exact from a friend's lips what he only knows

o

in confidence ?   Poor imprudent beings !   They have had their moments of sincerity : for this your sad civilisation of the West makes them pay with the rest of their broken lives.

.      .      .      .      .      .

For a long time I have wanted to make the acquaintance of Mr. W. T. Stead, who is known and respected in the East more perhaps than any Englishman.   I had no particular reason to go and see him except that he knew my father at the first Hague Conference.   So, one day I was bold enough to jump into a hansom and drive to his office.   I was asked whom I wanted.   I asked for Mr. Stead.

" Who wants him ? "  I was asked.

" I do," I replied.

" Give me your card."   But as I had no card I wrote on a slip of paper :  " The daughter of a Turkish friend of the Hague Conference will be so pleased to see you."

He received me at once.   There was so much to talk about.   He spoke so nicely of my poor dead father, questioned me about the Sultan, about the country I had left, about the Balkans, about Crete, and the Turks themselves.   More than an hour we talked together, and when finally I rose to go he said to me : " Is there anything I can do for you ? "

" No," I said, thanking him very kindly.

" Then it was simply to see me," he went on, " that you came."

" Yes," I said, " it is a friendly visit." He laughed heartily.

" Do you know," he said, " that is the first time that this has happened in my life."

Then he was kind enough to send for tea, and the tray was put down on the table among the papers and the journals, and he showed me signed portraits which he had collected during his travels, among them the one that my dear father had given him at The Hague. He then gave me his own, and signed it, " To my only Turkish lady friend."

.     .     .     .     .     .

I saw him for a little while in Paris on his return from Constantinople, and he came back really enthusiastic. He was much in sympathy with the Young Turks, though he had much also to find fault with. He despised but pitied Abdul Hamid, and hoped that an *entente* between England and Turkey could be arranged, but his ideas were quite unpractical. His policy was purely sentimental, and his suggestions impossible.

. . . . . .

I have had the pleasure, since I have been here, of seeing two diplomatists with whose voices I was familiar for many years in Constantinople. My father highly esteemed them both; they often came to see him. When they had drunk their coffee, sometimes my father sent for us to come and play and sing to them, and from behind a curtain they courteously thanked us for our performance.

Although I had so often heard their voices I never had an opportunity of seeing a photo of either of them, and I can't tell whether I was agreeably surprised or not. Have you ever tried putting a body to a voice?

. . . . . .

What a magnificent city London is! If you English are not proud of it, you ought to be. It is not only grand and magnificent but has an aristocratic look that despises mere ornament.

Here in London I have a feeling of security, which I have had nowhere else in the world. It is the only capital in Europe I have so far seen that gives me a sense of orderliness not dependent on authority. It seems to me as if English character were expressed even in the houses of the people. You can tell at a glance what kind of people dwell in the house you are entering. How different is Paris! What a delight to have no concierge, those petty potentates who, as it were, keep the key of your daily life, and remedy there is none.

For the first time since I left Turkey I have had here the sensation of real home life. As you know, we have no flats in Turkey, and have room to move about freely—room for your delightful English furniture, which to me is the most comfortable in the whole world.

Like ours, the houses here are made for use, and their wide doors and broad passages seem to extend a welcome to you which French houses hardly ever do. In France you smell economy before you even reach the door-mat.

You who are in Turkey can now understand what I have suffered from this narrowness of French domestic life. You can imagine my surprise when, the morning after my arrival here, a big tray was sent into my room with a heavy meal of eggs, bacon, fish, toast, marmalade, and what not. I thought I must have looked ill and as if I needed extra feeding, and I explained to my hostess that my white skin was not a sign of anæmia but my Oriental complexion : all the eggs and bacon in the world would not change the colour of my skin. She was not aware that the Mahometan never eats pork, and like so many others, seemed to forget that bacon, like pork, came from a forbidden source.

I do not find London noisy, but what noise there is one feels is serving a purpose. Life seems so serious ; everyone is busy crowding into twelve hours the work of twenty-four. We Turks take no heed of the passing hours.

The Englishmen remind me of the Turks. They have the same grave demeanour, the same appearance of indifference to our sex, the same look of stubborn determination, and, like the Turk, every Englishman is a Sultan in his own house. Like the Turk, too, he is sincere and faithful in his friendships, but Englishmen have two qualities that the Turks do not possess. They are extremely good business men, and in social relations are extremely prudent, although it is difficult to say where prudence ends and hypocrisy begins.

THE DRAWING-ROOM OF A HAREM SHOWING A BRIDAL THRONE

On the Bridal Throne the Turkish woman sits on her wedding day to receive her friends' good wishes. It remains the chief seat in the harem; in the Imperial Palace it is a fine throne, in poor houses only a glorified chair, but it is always there.

A CORNER OF THE HAREM

This Turkish lady collected the ribbons of the battleships on the Bosphorus, and they are hanging on the wall.

But if Englishmen remind me of Turks, I can find nothing in common between English and Turkish women. They are in direct contrast to one another in everything. Perhaps it is this marked contrast that balances our friendship. A Turkish woman's life is as mysterious as an Englishwoman's life is an open book, which all can read who care. Before I met the suffragettes, I knew only sporting and society women. They were all passionately absorbed in their own amusements, which as you know do not in the least appeal to me. I suppose we Turkish women who have so much time to devote to culture become unreasonably exacting. But everywhere I have been—in England, Germany, France, Italy, and Spain—I have found how little and how uselessly the women read, and how society plays havoc with their taste for good books.

Englishwomen are pretty, but are deficient in charm. They have no particular desire and make no effort to please. You know the charm of the Turkish woman. The Englishwoman is pig-headed, undiplomatic, brutally sincere, but a good and faithful friend. The Turkish woman—well, you must fill that in yourself! I am too near to focus her.

But now that I have seen the women of most countries, you may want to know which I most admire.

Well, I will tell you frankly, the Turkish woman. An ordinary person would answer, "Of course," but you are not an ordinary person, so I shall at once give you my reasons. It is not because I am a Turkish woman myself, but because, in spite of the slavery of their existence, Turkish women have managed to keep their minds free from prejudice. With them it is not what people think they ought to think, but what they think themselves. Nowhere else in Europe have I found women with such courage in thinking.

In every country there are women—though they may be a mere handful—who are above class, above nationality, and dare to be themselves. These are the people I appreciate the most. These are the people I shall always wish to know, for to them the whole world is kin.— Your affectionate friend, ZEYNEB.

# CHAPTER XIX

## IN THE ENEMY'S LAND

# CHAPTER XIX

## IN THE ENEMY'S LAND

VENICE, *Oct.* 1911.

YOU will say perhaps I am reminded of the Bosphorus everywhere, just as Maurice Barres is reminded of Lorraine in every land he visits. Yet how would it be possible not to think of the Bosphorus in Venice, especially when for so many years I have had to do without it ? Here, there is the same blue sky, the same blue carpet of sea, the same sunset, and the same wonderful sunrise —only gondolas have taken the place of caïques.

All day and part of the evening I allow myself to be rowed as my gondolier wishes from canal to canal, and I am indignant I did not know sooner there was a place in Europe where one could come to rest. Why do the French and Swiss doctors not send their patients here ? They would be cured certainly of that disease from which everyone suffers nowadays, the fatigue of the big towns.

But since so many illustrious poets have sung the praises of Venice what is there for me to say ?   I prefer to glorify it as the Brahmins worship their Deity, in silence.

The Venetians do not appreciate Venice any more than I appreciated Constantinople when I lived there.   They have no idea how lovely Venice is, but prefer the Lido, where they meet the people of all nations, whose buzzing in the daytime replaces the mosquitoes at night.

On our way here, the train went off the rails, so we had to alight for some time : then one of the party suggested that we should visit Verona, and I was very delighted at this happy idea.

It was midnight.   We walked along the narrow streets of the deserted city.   The town was bathed in a curious, indescribable light, and it was more beautiful than anything we could have seen in the daylight, when perhaps the noise would have killed its charm.   I hope that fate has not decreed that my impression of that silent sleeping city shall ever be destroyed.

I travelled to Venice in a compartment marked " Ladies only," not because I have any particular affection for those " harem " compartments, but because there was not a seat for me with my friends. An old English spinster was my companion. She welcomed me with a graciousness that I did not appreciate, and at once began a very dull and conventional conversation.

Presently, however, two Italian officers came in, and politely excusing themselves in their language, sat down. They said they had been up all night, had been standing from Milan, and had to go on duty when they reached Venice, and begged the old lady politely to allow them a quarter of an hour's rest.

The spinster did not understand, so I translated.

"Disgraceful," she said and ordered them out. But still the officers remained. Then turning to me she said, "You who must be Italian, please tell them what I think of them."

I told her, "It was not my rôle to interpret such uncharitable language."

Then the officers turning to me, said in Italian, "Although English, you are much kinder than your companion; please tell her we only want to stop a quarter of an hour, and there is absolutely no danger for her."

Rising, the old spinster looked for the alarm signal, but finally decided to call the guard, who ordered the officers out. Before they went, however, they pulled out their watches and asked me to thank her for her kind hospitality: they reminded me that they had what they wanted, a quarter of an hour's rest.

Luckily our arrival at Venice meant good-bye to this disagreeable old creature, whose type flourishes all over the Continent, even in Constantinople, and who sacrifices on the altar of respectability everything, even charity.

.        .        .        .        .        .

Now I understand the enthusiasm of those who have spoken of Italy. Nothing one can say is sufficient eulogy for this land of sunshine and poetry and tradition.

I am told by the people of the north I shall be disappointed when I see the south, but that does not disturb my impression of the moment. I am worshipping Venice, and everything there pleases me.

To me it seems almost as if it were the home of the ancient Greeks, with all their artistic instincts and roguery, all their faults, and all their primitive charm. From my open window, which looks into a canaletto, I heard the song of a gondolier. His voice was the sweetest I

A Caïque on the Bosphorus

Turkish Women in the Country

have ever heard ; no opera singer ever gave me greater pleasure. Now that I know the number of his boat, I have engaged him as my gondolier, and every evening after dinner, instead of wasting my time at Bridge, I go on to the canal, leaving it to the discretion of my guide where he takes me ; and when he is tired of rowing, he brings me back. All the time he sings and sings and I dream, and his beautiful voice takes me far, far away—away from the unfriendly West.

Amongst its other attractions, Venice has an aristocracy. They are poor certainly, but, with such blood in their veins, do they need riches ? And surely their charm and nobility are worth all the dollars put together of the vulgar Transatlantics who have bought the big historic palaces of Venice. I feel here as I felt in London, the delight of being again in a Kingdom, and I can breathe and live. How restful it is, after the nervous strain of the exaggerated Democracy of France.

.    .    .    .    .    .

BRUSSELS, *Nov.* 1911.

I have had this letter quite a fortnight in my trunk. I did not want to send it to you. Some-how I felt ashamed to let you see how much I had loved Italy—Turkey's enemy.

I left Venice the day after the Declaration of War, if such a disgraceful proceeding would be called a Declaration of War. For a long time I could not make up my mind that that nation of gentlemen, that nation of poetry and music and art, that nation whose characteristics so appealed to my Oriental nature, that nation whom I thought so civilised in the really good sense of the word, could be capable of such injustice.

Even in the practice of "the rights of the strong" a little more tact could have been exercised. Surely it is not permissible in the twentieth century to act as savages did—at least those we thought savages.

In a few years from now, we shall be able to see more clearly how the Italian Government of 1911 was able to step forward and take advantage of a Sister State, whose whole efforts were centred on regeneration, and no one protested. What a wonderful account of the history of our times !

When I think that it is in Christian Europe that such injustice passes unheeded, and that

Christian Europe dares to send us missionaries to preach this gospel of Civilisation—I curse the Fate which has forced me to accept the hospitality of the West.

.     .     .     .     .     .

Two chapters more seem necessary to my experience of the West. I submit in silence. Kismet.

Hardly had I returned from Brussels than I became seriously ill. Do not ask me what was the matter with me. Science has not yet found a name for my suffering. I have consulted doctors, many doctors, and perhaps for this reason I have no idea as to the nature of my illness. Each doctor wanted to operate for something different, and only when I told them I had not the money for an operation have they found that after all it is not necessary. I think I have internal neuralgia, but modern science calls it " appendicitis," and will only treat me under that fashionable name. At Smyrna, I remember having a similar attack. My grandmother, terrified to see me suffering, ran in for a neighbour whom she knew only by name. The

P

neighbour came at once, said a few prayers over me, passed her magic hands over my body, and in a short time I was healed.

Here I might have knocked up all the inhabitants of Paris : not one would have come to help me.

" The progress of modern science " was my last illusion. Why must I have this final disappointment ? Yet what does it matter ? Every cloud has a silver lining. And this final experience has brought me to the decision, that I shall go back to Turkey as soon as I can walk. There at least, unless my own people have been following in the footsteps of modern civilisation, I shall be allowed to be ill at my leisure, without the awful spectre hovering over me of a useless operation.

One night I was suffering so much that I thought it advisable to send for the doctor. It was only two o'clock in the morning, but the message the concierge sent back was, " that one risked being assassinated in Paris at that hour," and he refused to go.

The next day I had a letter from my landlord requesting me not to wake the concierge up again at two o'clock in the morning. And this is the country of liberty, the country where one is free to die, provided only the concierge is not awakened at two o'clock in the morning.

This little incident seems insignificant in itself, but to me it will be a very painful remembrance of one of the chief characteristics of the people of this country—a total lack of hospitality.

If our Oriental countries must one day become like these countries of the West, if they too must inherit all the vices, with which this civilisation is riddled through and through, then let them perish now.

If civilisation does not teach each individual the great and supreme quality of pity, then what use is it ?  What difference is there, please tell me, between the citizens of Paris and the carnivorous inhabitants of Darkest Africa ?  We Orientals imagine the word civilisation is a synonym of many qualities, and I, like others, believed it.  Is it possible to be so primitive ?  Yet why should I be ashamed of believing in the goodness of human beings ?  Why should I blame myself, because these people have not come up to my expectations ?

This musing reminds me of a story which our Koran Professor used to tell us.  " There was

once," he said, " in a country of Asia Minor, a
little girl who believed all she heard.  One day
she looked out of her window, and saw a chain
of mountains blue in the distance.

" ' Is that really their colour ? ' she asked her
comrades.

" ' Yes,' they answered.

" And so delighted was she with this information that she started out to get a nearer view
of the blue mountains.

" Day after day she walked and walked, and
at last got to the summit of the blue mountains,
only to find grass just as she would have found
it anywhere else.  But she would not give up.

" ' Where are the blue mountains ? ' she asked
a shepherd, and he showed another chain higher
and farther away, and on and on she went until
she came to the mountains of Alti.

" All her existence she had the same hopes
and the same illusions.  Only when she came to
the evening of her life did she understand that
it was the distance that lent the mountains their
hue—but it was too late to go back, and she
perished in the cold, biting snow."

.    .    .    .    .    .

I do not know if there is another country in

MELEK ON THE VERANDA AT FONTAINEBLEAU

the world where foreigners can be as badly treated as they are here; at any rate they could not be treated worse. They are criticised, laughed at, envied, and flattered, and they have the supreme privilege of paying for all those people whose hobby is economy.

Everything is done here by paradox; the foreigner who has talent is more admired than the Frenchman, yet if he does anything wrong, there is no forgiveness for him.

An Englishwoman I knew quarrelled with a Frenchwoman, and the latter reproached her with having accepted one luncheon and one dinner. The Englishwoman (it sounds fearfully English, doesn't it?) sent her ex-hostess twelve francs, and the Frenchwoman not only accepted it but sent a receipt. If I had not seen that receipt I don't think I could have believed the story!

Another lady, whose dressmaker claimed from her a sum she was not entitled to, was told by that dressmaker, unless she were paid at once, she would inform the concierge. Tell me, I beg of you, in what other country would this have been possible? In what other country of the world would self-respecting people pay any attention, far less go for information, to the vulgar harpies who preside over the destinies of the fifteen or twenty families who occupy a Paris house ?

When I have been able to get my ideas and impressions a little into focus, I intend to write for you, and for you only, what a woman without any preparation for the battle of life, a foreigner, a woman alone, and last but not least, a Turk, has had to suffer in Paris.

You who know what our life is in Turkey, and how we have been kept in glass cases and wrapt in cotton wool, with no knowledge of the meaning of life, will understand what the awful change means, and how impossible for a Turkish woman is Western life.

Do you remember the year of my arrival? Do you remember how I wanted to urge all my young friends away yonder to take their liberty as I had taken mine, so that before they died they might have the doubtful pleasure of knowing what it was to live ?

Now, I hope if ever they come to Europe they will not come to Paris except as tourists ; that they will see the beautiful things there are to be seen, the Provence with its fine cathedrals and its historic surroundings; that they will amuse themselves taking motor-car trips and comparing it with their excursions on a mule's back in Asia; that they will see the light of Paris, but never its shade; and that they will return, as you have returned from Constantinople, with one regret, that you couldn't stay longer.

If only my experience could be of use to my compatriots who are longing as I longed six years ago for the freedom of the West, I shall never regret having suffered.—Your affectionate friend, ZEYNEB.

# CHAPTER XX
## THE END OF THE DREAM

# CHAPTER XX

## THE END OF THE DREAM

MARSEILLES, 5th March, 1912.

IT is to-morrow that I sail. In a week from to-day, I shall again be away yonder amongst those whom I have always felt so near, and who I know have not forgotten me.

In just a week from to-day I shall again be one of those unrecognisible figures who cross and recross the silent streets of our town—some one who no longer belongs to the same world as you—some one who must not even think as you do—some one who will have to try and forget she led the existence of a Western woman for six long, weary years.

What heart-breaking disappointments have I not to take away with me ! It makes me sad to think how England has changed ! England with its aristocratic buildings and kingly archi-tecture—England with its proud and self-respecting democracy—the England that our great Kemal Bey taught us to know, that splendid people the world admires so much, sailing so dangerously near the rocks.

I do not pretend to understand the suffra-gettes or their " window-smashing " policy, but I must say, I am even more surprised at the attitude of your Government. However much these ill-advised women have over-stepped the boundaries of their sex privileges, however wrong they may be, surely the British Govern-ment could have found some other means of dealing with them, given their cause the atten-tion they demanded, or used some diplomatic way of keeping them quiet. I cannot tell you the horrible impression it produces on the mind of a Turkish woman to learn that England not only imprisons but tortures women ; to me it is the cataclysm of all my most cherished faiths. Ever since I can remember, England had been to me a kind of Paradise on earth, the land which welcomed to its big hospitable bosom all Europe's political refugees. It was the land of all lands I longed to visit, and now I hear a Liberal Government is torturing women. Some-how my mind will not accept this statement.

Write to me often, very often, dear girl.

You know exactly where I shall be away yonder, and exactly what I shall be doing. You know even the day when I shall again begin my quiet, almost cloistered existence as a Moslem woman, and how I shall long for news of that Europe which has so interested and so disappointed me.

Do you remember with what delight I came to France, the country of Liberté, Egalité, and Fraternité ? But now I have seen those three magic words in practice, how the whole course of my ideas has changed! Not only are my theories on the nature of governments no longer the same, but my confidence in the individual happiness that each can obtain from these governments is utterly shattered.

But you will say, I argue like a reactionary. Let me try to explain. Am I not now a woman of experience, a woman of six years' experience, which ought to count as double, for every day has brought me a double sensation, the one of coming face to face with the reality, and the other, the effort of driving from my mind the remembrance of what I expected to find ?

You know how I loved the primitive soul of the people, how I sympathise with them, and how I hoped that some scheme for the betterment of their condition would be carried out.

But I expected in France the same good honest Turks I knew in our Eastern villages, and it was from the Eastern simplicity and loyalty that I drew my conclusions about the people of the West. You know now what they are! And do not for a moment imagine that I am the only one to make this mistake: nine out of ten of my compatriots, men and women, would have the same expectation of them. Until they have come to the West to see for themselves and had some of the experiences that we have had, they will never appreciate the calm, leisurely people of our country.

How dangerous it is to urge those Orientals forward, only to reduce them in a few years to the same state of stupidity as the poor degenerate peoples of the West, fed on unhealthy literature and poisoned with alcohol.

You are right: it is in the West that I have learned to appreciate my country. Here I have studied its origin, its history (and I still know only too little of it), but I shall take away with me very serious knowledge about Turkey.

But again I say, what a disappointment the

West has been. Yes, taking it all round I must own that I am again a *désenchantée*. Do you know, I am now afraid even of a charwoman who comes to work for me. Alas! I have learned of what she is capable—theft, hatred, vengeance, and the greed of money, for which she would sell her soul.

I told the editor of a Paris paper one day that I blushed at the manner in which he encouraged dirty linen to be washed in public. "All your papers are the same," I said. "Take them one after the other and see if one article can be found which is favourable to your poor country. You give the chief place to horrible crimes. Your leading article contains something scandalous about a minister, and from these articles France is judged not only by her own people but by the whole world."

He did not contradict me, but smiling maliciously, he answered, "Les journalistes ont *à cœur* d'être aussi veridique que possible." ("Journalists must try to be as truthful as possible.") A clever phrase, perhaps, but worse than anything he could have written in the six pages of his paper.

But perhaps I am leaving you under the impression, *désenchantée* though I be, that nothing has pleased me in the West. Not at all! I have many delightful impressions to take back with me, and I want to return some day if the " Kismet " will allow it.

Munich, Venice, the Basque Countries, the Riviera, and London I hope to see again. Art and music, the delightful libraries, the little towns where I have worked, thought, and discovered so many things, and a few friends " who can understand "—surely these are attractions great enough to bring me back to Europe again.

The countries I have seen are beautiful enough, but civilisation has spoiled them. To take a copy of what it was going to destroy, however, civilisation created art—art in so many forms, art in which I had revelled in the West. It was civilisation that collected musical harmonies, civilisation that produced Wagner, and music to my mind is the finest of all its works.

But there are books too, you will say, wonderful books. Yes, but in the heart of Asia there are quite as many masterpieces, and they are far more reposeful.

.    .    .    .    .    .

This morning early I was wakened by the sun, the advance-guard of what I expect away yonder. From my window I see a portion of the harbour, and the curious ships which start and arrive from all corners of the earth. Again I see the Bosphorus with its ships, which in my childish imagination were fairy godmothers who would one day take me far, far away . . . and now they are the fairy godmothers who will take me back again.

I like to watch this careless, boisterous, gay crowd of Marseilles. It is just a little like the port of Échelles du Levant with its variegated costumes, its dirt, which the sun makes bearable, and the continual cries and quarrelling among men of all nations.

All my trunks are packed and ready, and it is with joy and not without regret that I see I have no hatbox. Not that I care for that curious and very unattractive invention, the fashionable hat, but it is the external symbol of liberty, and now I am setting it aside for ever. My *tchatchaff* is ready, and once we have passed the Piræus I shall put it on. How strange I shall feel clad again from head to foot in a black mantle all out of fashion, for the Turks have narrowed their *tchatchaffs* as the Western women have tightened their skirts. It will not be without emotion, either, that I feel a black veil over my face, a veil between me and the sun, a veil to prevent me from seeing it as I saw it for the first time at Nice from my wide open window.

Yet what anguish, what terrible anguish would it not be for me to put on that veil again, if I did not hope to see so many of those I have really loved, the companions of my childhood, friends I know who wanted me and have missed me. Even when I left Constantinople, you know under what painful circumstances, I hoped to return one day.

" The world is a big garden which belongs to us all," said a Turkish warrior of the past; " one must wander about and gather its most agreeable fruits as one will." Ah! the holy philosophy! yet how far are we from ever attempting to understand it! Will there ever come a personality strong enough, with a voice powerful enough to persuade us that this philosophy is for our sovereign being, and that without it we shall be led and lead others to disappointments ?

During the time I was away yonder, I believed in the infallibility of new theories. I had almost completely neglected the books of our wise men of the East, but I have read them in the libraries of the West, where I have neglected modern literature for the pleasure of studying that philosophy, which shows the vanity of these struggles and the suffering that can follow.

I am longing to see an old uncle from the Caucasus. When we were young girls he pitied us because we were so unarmed against the disenchantment which inevitably had to come to us.

" You are of another century," we said to him. " You reason with theories you find remarkable, but we want to go forward, we want to fight for progress, and that is only right."

Ah ! he knew what he was talking about, that old uncle, when he spoke of the disenchantment of life.

" You are arguing as I argued when I was a little boy, and my father gave me the answer that I have given to you. My children," he continued, " life does not consist in always asking for more : believe me, there is more merit in living happily on as little as you can, than in struggling to rise on the defeat of others. I have fought in all the battles against the

Russians, and had great experience of life, but I remind you of the fact merely lest you should think me a vulgar fatalist in the hands of destiny. I, too, have had many struggles, and it was my duty."

What a lot I shall have to tell this dear old uncle! How well we shall understand each other now, how happy he will be to see that I have understood him! We shall speak in that language which I need to speak again after six long years. Loving the East to fanaticism as I do, to me it stands for all that glorious past which the younger generation should appreciate but not blame, all the past with which I find myself so united.

I will tell this dear old uncle (and indeed am I not as old and experienced as he?) that I love my country to-day as I never loved it before, and if only I may be able to prove this I shall ask nothing more of life.

.    .    .    .    .    .

NAPLES.

I can only write you a few lines to-day. The sea has been so rough that many of the passengers have preferred to remain on board. Some one impertinently asked me if I were afraid to go on shore, but I did not answer, having too much to say. Around me I hear the language which once I spoke with such delight; now it has become odious to me, as odious as that Italy which I have buried like a friend of the past.

Now there is a newspaper boy on board crying with rapture "Another Italian victory." He offers me a paper. I want to shout my hatred of his country, I want to call from Heaven the vengeance of Allah on these cowardly Italians, but my tongue is tied and my lips will not give utterance to the thoughts I feel. I stand like one dazed.

Surely these accounts of victory are false. Are not these reports prepared beforehand to give courage to the Italian soldiers in their glorious mission of butchering the Turks, those fine valiant men who will stand up for their independence as long as a man remains to fight?

At last I go and lock myself in my cabin, so as not to hear their hateful jubilation, but they follow me even to my solitude. Some one knocks. Reluctantly I open. It is a letter. But there must be some error. Who can have written to me when I particularly asked that I should have no letters until I arrived?

But the letter came from Turkey, and the Turkish stamp almost frightened me : for a long time I had not the courage to open it. When at last I slowly cut the envelope of that letter, I found it contained the cutting of a newspaper which announced the death of the dear old uncle whom more than anyone I was longing to see again.

Outside the conquerors were crying out, even louder than before, " More Turkish losses, more Turkish losses." I folded up the letter and put it back in its envelope with a heart too bitter for tears.

.     .     .     .     .     .

What did it all mean ? What was the warning that fate was sending to me in this cruel manner ? *Désenchantée* I left Turkey, *désenchantée* I have left Europe. Is that rôle to be mine till the end of my days ?—Your affectionate friend, ZEYNEB.

Printed by BALLANTYNE, HANSON & CO.
Edinburgh & London

For EU product safety concerns, contact us at Calle de José Abascal, 56–1°,
28003 Madrid, Spain or eugpsr@cambridge.org.